LIVE ISSUES

ALSO BY MAVIS KLEIN

Lives People Live
How to Choose a Mate
Discover Your Real Self
Understanding Your Child
Pain and Joy in Intimate Relationships

LIVE ISSUES

Reflections on
the Human Condition

Mavis Klein

Ad Astra Books
Cambridge, England

Ad Astra Books, 21 Lady Jane Court,
Cavendish Avenue, Cambridge CB1 7UW
telephone/fax: 01223 412830

First published in Great Britain
By Ad Astra Books, 2003

British Library Cataloguing in Publication Data
A catalogue record for this book is available from the
British Library.

ISBN 0-9543989-0-4

Printed and bound in Great Britain by
Black Bear Press Limited
King's Hedges Road Cambridge CB4 2PQ

For Maia, Leila, Helena and
Benjamin – and to life

CONTENTS

DEUTERONOMY – HERE AND NOW

ACKNOWLEDGEMENTS

The contents of this book were simmering amorphously in my mind when, in March 2002, Ian Lee invited me to contribute a 150 word column to a magazine he edits. I so enjoyed writing in that straightjacket that I instantly decided to apply it to my book.

Later, Ian Lee generously gave me the benefits of his talents as both copywriter and graphic designer. He thought of the title, serendipitously saw the correspondence between my essays and the first five books of the Old Testament, designed the cover, and wrote its copy.

I am grateful to Christina Rodenbeck whose meticulous editing of my typescript vastly enhanced the coherence and readability of the whole; to Ros Saunders who cheerfully designed the inside of the book at a moment's notice; and to Maureen and Michael Joseph who gave me valuable practical advice from their know-how in the businesses of publishing and bookselling.

INTRODUCTION

This book is informed by my love of philosophical, psychological and spiritual theories of the human condition, and my desire to share with a wide public those theories that I have tried and tested over many years and which continue to delight me.

My first two loves were the apparently irreconcilably mutually hostile psychological theories of Freud and B.F.Skinner; but they found their perfect reconciliation for me in my third love, Transactional Analysis, which has been my *lingua franca* as a psychotherapist for the past 28 years. Then came astrology, which blew my mind and spirit wide open and which, I believe, is the queen of all conceptualizations ever construed by humankind. But I now use all these languages in parallel rather than in combat in everyday life.

Most serious books are thought marathons; this serious book is a collection of thought sprints. I hope they set your pulse racing.

TERMINOLOGY

While each of the mini-essays in this book is essentially
self-sufficient, I have made use of a few shorthand terms
for complex but easily understood concepts. These are
progressively introduced in the sections Human Nature
and Personality Types. Readers who choose for
themselves to dip, unbound, into the later essays first will
probably find the meanings of the few jargon terms used
easy to infer in their contexts. If not, reference to the
early essays will quickly clarify their meanings.

The terms Parents, Adult and Child "ego states", "games"
and "strokes" are the legacy of Eric Berne, the genius
who developed the overall theory of Transactional
Analysis. The five basic and ten compound personality
types are my own development of Transactional Analysis
out of 20 years psychotherapeutic practice. I am
especially indebted to my TA colleague, Taibi Kahler,
whose original "miniscript" theory was the launch pad for
my own originality.

Genesis

HUMAN NATURE

THE RULES OF THE GAME

Eric Berne was an American psychoanalyst who, in the 1950s and 1960s, developed Transactional Analysis out of his dissatisfaction with the slowness of psychoanalysis as therapy.

Psychoanalysis justifies its slowness in the name of the necessarily prolonged process of accessing our infantile memories in order to resolve our neurotic conflicts. Berne argued that this process is unnecessary and that here and now consciousness is quite sufficient material out of which our deepest problems can be accessed, addressed, and resolved. He remained, however, completely loyal to psychoanalysis as a theory of child development and psychopathology, so Transactional Analysis (TA) became essentially 'Freud without the unconscious'.

Forty years on, TA remains an enormously popular psychological language and is widely used in educational and business contexts as well as in psychotherapy. Berne's concept of 'games', as described in his best-seller *Games People Play*, is widely used by many people quite unfamiliar with his work.

IN THE BEGINNING

The first rule of human consciousness is that everywhere in the universe duality reigns. It is by pairs of opposites that we apprehend the world, and find it uncomfortable; and, consciously or not, we struggle towards the primeval unity that we infer was once and will be again a state of bliss. Here, approximately in order, are our most important dualities.

Order and chaos (His first division); night and day; male and female; arousal and quiescence; good and evil; guilt and innocence; life and death; murder and suicide; immortal (those whose parents are alive) and mortal (those whose parents are dead); heaven and hell; loving and hating; loving and being loved; loving and being indifferent; analysis and synthesis.

All opposites seek their resolution through a third entity that reunifies them. Most gloriously, love and death are united in sexual orgasm and deep laughter can joyfully conflagrate any and all dualities.

DESIRE

We are homeostatic organisms, inescapably swinging between arousal and quiescence for as long as we are alive. We apply thousands of words to this basic dichotomy with which we elaborate it into a large range of evaluated discrete experiences, depending largely on context. Being aroused, when we haven't eaten for five hours becomes "hungry"; in response to a threatening stimulus "frightened"; in anticipation of fulfilled desire "excited"; to the blocking of desire "frustrated"; to the unexpected blocking of desire "disappointed".

Pleasure is the transitional moment of quiescence consequent on the fulfillment of desire, before the memory of the desire is quite faded and before the movement that is called being alive propels us into the chase after another desire. Desire seeks its fulfillment in pleasure, but pleasure is not guaranteed. Intrinsic to the process is the risk of failure and an associated degree of pain equivalent to the pleasure sought.

PARADOX

Paradoxically, all opposites, which usually keep each other in check, when escalated to the critical degree, implode in unitary self-destructiveness; and all bipolar dimensions in our lives are ultimately derivatives of the primary ones of arousal and quiescence. Too much arousal leads to danger which, in extremis, leads to death; perfect stillness is death.

Our pleasures are all contained in the transitory moments of achieved harmony between order and chaos, being and doing, safety and adventure, certainty and risk, organization and efficiency, thought and action, commitment and freedom, self-control and self-indulgence, inhibition and spontaneity, penny-pinching and extravagance, depression and mania, righteousness and paranoia, sureness and doubt, self-denial and greed, caution and bravado, meaningfulness and meaninglessness – from the smallest of the largest episodes in our lives.

Maximum pleasure for extraverts is associated with relatively large amounts of arousing stimulation; maximum pleasure for introverts is associated with relatively large amounts of quiescence.

TIME AND MONEY

Contemporary cosmologists in their bid to evade the child's deep question, 'Who made God?' or its grown-up version, 'What was there before the Big Bang?' say this is a meaningless question because Time only came into being with the Big Bang. Einstein famously proved that time is relative to the observer and our ordinary experience of the linear flow of time, with causes succeeded by effects, may be a fiction; which hypothesis is supported by the accumulated evidence of pre-cognition.

But in the ordinary realm of human consciousness time and its flow, from the known past through ungraspable present to indeterminate future, is a pervasive reality woven into the fabric of our being.

Money, too, (or its bartering equivalent) is an invention necessary in our quotidian lives, and each individual in his or her idiosyncratic way construes and relates to money in exactly the same way as (s)he does to time.

SPENDING

We *spend* both time and money which are necessary central constructs around which we weave our quotidian lives. Paradoxically, we are happiest when we are least aware of them. Our experience of having more than enough as well as less than enough of either or both of them disturbs our equanimity. Optimally, we have enough of each to meet our survival needs and a little bit extra to play with.

There are five discrete ways in which people apprehend and spend time and money:

> Making and saving time and money
> Using time and money
> Passing time and frittering money
> Squandering time and money
> Killing time and losing money

These five ways are specific manifestation of five deep existential decisions by which people live their lives – decisions which are made very early in life and are virtually immutable. They are presented in five singular and ten compound pairs of personality types.

BALANCING ACTS

Time, money, planning and effort are deeply entrenched constructs in the human mind, against the backdrop of which, however, unconsciously, we run our lives.

Time and money are equated in association with arousal; and planning and effort are equated in association with quiescence. Is the time saved by getting a taxi rather than a bus *worth* the extra money? Is the money I can save buying my groceries at a distant supermarket *worth* the time it takes to get there and back instead of using my corner shop? How much effort saved is *worth* planning a week's meals in advance? How much planning is it *worth* saving for the effort of finding my way around a new city by trial and error?

We are constantly exchanging time and money and planning and effort; but each individual leads her overall life from a relatively stable position on the overall dimension of arousal-quiescence.

CIVILIZATION AND CULTURE

Whether or not there has been or can be progress in matters pertaining to human nature is debatable. Civilization is the usual name given to the structures of society that aim to increase the average overall happiness of the world. But these structures seem to be eminently fragile. Regular episodic outbursts of collective, uncivilized aggression seem to increase the average overall pain in the world in exact proportion to the degree of civilization that is the current ideal. It is arguable that the sum total of pleasure and pain in the world must, because of the immutability of human nature, remain constant. As sons and daughters of Adam and Even, we are all exiles from paradise.

Our consciousness of the imperfection of our human nature and our valiant struggles to perfect ourselves sets us apart from all other species and has amongst its spin-offs all of art, science and philosophy.

FIGHT AND SURVIVAL

Reduced to its essence, human life is a desperate bid to deny or to find compensation for the fact that we must die. To this extent we live most authentically and contentedly when we are explicitly fighting for our survival. But with full stomachs and in peace-time we need to find causes and problems that serve as displacements of our basic quest for physical survival. Struggling, fighting, and succeeding in overcoming our problems distracts us from facing our mortality head-on.

All races and cultures throughout history have found in the quest to love and be loved the fantasied panacea against the actuality of death. But the game of love is universally and timelessly fraught with vulnerability and pain proportional to the joy that is being sought, which makes it a primary focus of our fight for survival in our increasingly affluent and peaceful (at least in our back yards) world.

FILTERING FACTS

The existence of our sense organs determines that we cannot avoid being constantly bombarded with facts; and our physical and psychological survival in the material world and the world of people necessitates our collecting and interpreting clusters of facts into theories, which we call the truth. Though the number of facts in the universe is infinite, once we have experienced and interpreted into truth a sufficient number of facts about matters pertaining to our continued existence in the context of our personal environments, we stop. Thereafter our minds filter out the information received by our sense organs that is not relevant to or contradict the theories we have formulated. By about the age of six, to all intents and purposes, our minds are permanently closed and nearly every experience we subsequently allow ourselves to have is a recapitulation, literally or metaphorically, of evidence for the truths we have established.

GOOD AND EVIL

The first facts we experience after birth, out of which we create a truth, are our bodily experiences of contentment and pain. Contentment becomes good and pain becomes bad.

Soon we realize that our attempts to eliminate pain from our lives are doomed to failure, and this becomes another fact that needs to be made sense of by theory. That is, we require a meta-theory that explains how the pain we experience is necessary. So the second essential theory we formulate invariably construes good and evil forces that permeate the universe. The unavoidable corollary to this truth is that, inasmuch as we are part and parcel of the universe, the good and evil forces of the universe must also be in us.

Thus are religion and morality born; and we spend the rest of our lives attempting to maintain our goodness by projecting badness onto other people or the universe.

PSYCHOLOGICAL REALITY

All sane people within a culture share more or less congruent theories about physical reality. True, an artist may see 'nothing but' colours and shapes, a banker will focus on the economic aspects of reality, and a naturalist may find city streets 'empty'; but we all respect the law of gravity, know the dangers of cars and fires, that yellow and blue make green … and a thousand other facts.

Out of our confident and confirmed agreement with others about physical reality we tend falsely to assume our agreement concerning psychological reality. True, there are overlaps between people's psychological realities or we would all be isolated in eternal autism. But, by and large, our psychological realities are as diverse as our physical realities are similar, being based on the huge variety of possible early emotional experiences out of which we each formulate our personal theories of human relationships.

MIND BOMBS

Our minds finely filter out stimuli that are incompatible with our established beliefs about reality. But our minds are not completely closed.

Firstly, facts incompatible with our beliefs may insistently refuse to go away. Occasionally, in human history, an Einstein challenges a Newton and, despite our denials, ridicule and inquisitions, when its time has come, the new idea will be heard and reality is extended or transformed. Individuals, too, may rarely have mind-blowing experiences – usually profoundly traumatic – that permanently alter their deepest theories of reality.

Secondly, we all desire to experience again the excitement of our earliest years before we had yet chosen the life-preserving truths we would live by. For this, we flirt with death – physically or mentally – from the thrills of rock climbing, motor racing, or riding the big dipper, to courses in philosophy that challenge us to realize that all knowledge and beliefs are tenuously 'not proven'.

MENTAL WEIRDNESS

The existence of *idiot savants* and some autistic children imply some fascinating questions about all our brains.

Idiot savants are severely mentally retarded people who also have particular capacities incredibly greater than even the most intelligent of the rest of us. Their special ability is usually in arithmetical calculations, such as faultlessly and nearly instantaneously naming the day of the week of any date past or present. Some autistic children have the equally incredible ability to observe a landscape or cityscape for a few seconds and then reproduce it as a drawing, accurate to the minutest detail.

What is the connection between these people's handicaps and talents? Could the rest of us gain these (or other) talents by forfeiting part of our normal functioning? Is there a zero-sum equation between all our handicaps and talents and, if so, how is this represented in the anatomy and physiology of our brains?

EGO STATES

In TA, our personalities are comprised of three components, the Parent, Adult and Child ego states. These are states of being amongst which we move throughout our waking lives. Each has a structure and a function.

Our Parent ego state contains our beliefs and values, its function being to control and protect ourselves and others against impetuousness. Our Adult ego state contains our objective knowledge and skills, its function being to collect and compute information. Our Child ego state contains our innate and conditioned feelings, its function being to express itself.

People vary in the relative dominance of each ego state in their total personalities, which accounts for human variety. But our psychological health and effectiveness is related to our ability to be appropriately in one or other of our ego states – in our Parent when signing a petition, Our Adult when doing our accounts, in our Child at a party.

STROKES

A stroke, in TA, is any act of recognition that one human being gives another. We require a regular supply of strokes as much as we require food for our survival.

There are unconditional positive and negative strokes – "I love you whatever you do to please or displease me" and "I hate you, no matter what you do to win my approval." And conditional positive and negative strokes – "I'll buy you a new pair of jeans if you tidy up your room", and "Do that once more and I'll wallop you". If we can't get positive strokes we would rather get negative strokes – a kick, a put-down – than no strokes at all.

The prototype of all positive strokes is the unconditionally loving skin to skin contact we experienced at our mothers' breasts. The closest we get to this in adult life is the ecstasy of sexual orgasm with a loving other.

TRANSACTIONS

Strokes are given and received in transactions between the Parent, Adult or Child or one person and the Parent, Adult or Child of another.

Examples:

'We must put a kid-proof lock on this bathroom cabinet.' (Parent to Parent)

'Could you tell me the time?' (Adult to Adult)

'I love/hate you.' (Child to Child)

'May I have another biscuit?' (Child to Parent)

'Yes, you may.' (Parent to Child)

Pupil to teacher: 'What shall I do next?' (Adult to Parent)

'Here, let me show you how to tie shoelaces.' (Parent to Adult)

Girl to boy: 'You're so clever.' (Child to Adult)

Mother to whining toddler: 'Don't cry, we'll soon be home and you can have some lunch and a nice rest.' (Adult to Child)

But tone can override content in defining which ego state is speaking and which is being addressed. Try saying, 'What's for supper?' in each of the nine ways.

COMBINED EGO STATES

Functionally, the healthy adult is one who has his or her three ego states well-developed and differentiated and is also able to bring them into effective collaboration.

The Parent and Adult between them form judgements, the Parent and Child form compromises, and the Adult and Child find creative alternatives. And in all really important matters in our lives – getting married or divorced, moving house, changing jobs – we usually need the harmonious cooperation of all our ego state for the outcome of our decisions to be satisfactory.

It is probably for this reason that traditional education, from the ancient Greeks to our present day emphasizes the importance of physical games, which are excellent devices for training effective collaboration of our ego states. When a boy is playing football his Parent is obeying the rules, his Adult skills and competence are being exercised and his Child is having a marvellous time!

PREJUDICE, DELUSION, CONFUSION

Functional pathology is evident when an individual either does not have access to a particular ego state when its use is appropriately called for, or when the attempted collaboration of two ego states fails. Commonly, two ego states get 'contaminated' in an inauthentic, get-nowhere bind.

Parent-Adult contaminations are *prejudice*. E.g. a (Parent) belief that 'all Jews are rich' collides with the (Adult) reality of a very poor Jew in, 'He's the exception that proves the rule.'

Adult-Child contaminations are *delusions*. E.g. a (Child) desire to be loved by a particular man, who in (Adult) reality doesn't even notice me becomes, 'He must be in love with me or he wouldn't ignore me the way he does.'

Parent-Child contaminations are *confusion*. E.g. a (Child) desire for a dress I can't afford (Parent wants dutifully to pay the gas bill) is expressed in seeking the buy the dress with an unsigned cheque.

DISSOCIATION

The severest form of functional pathology occurs when the struggle to resolve difficult disagreements between our ego states is evaded by dissociation. That is, one or two ego states are suppressed out of consciousness to make the problem go away. The problem remains unresolved and this avoidance of it pays the very heavy price of decommissioning of the whole suppressed ego state.

The *uncaring* person is the one whose Parent is largely excluded.

The *turbulent person* is one whose Adult is largely excluded.

The *joyless person* is one whose Child is largely excluded.

The effective exclusion of two ego states from an individual's functioning is the most impoverishing defence of all against unresolved impasses between ego states.

The *harsh or smothering person* is the one who excludes his Adult and Child.

The *cold person* is the one who excludes his Parent and Child.

The *infantile person* is the one who excludes his Parent and Adult.

SELF-REVELATION

Human beings are metaphorical and symbolic creatures, and some of our deepest individual truths are discoverable through universal metaphors. Ask anybody the following questions to reveal their deepest idiosyncratic realities. Reveal yourself to yourself by answering the questions before reading the interpretative key.

In a few words describe your favourite animal (or bird or fish).

In a few words describe your second favourite animal (or bird or fish).

In a few words describe the sun.

In a few words describe the sea.

1) reveals our self-perception; 2) reveals our ego-ideal and the kind of people we are drawn to love; 3) reveals our present and/or childhood experience of home; 4) reveals our truth about sex.

The beauty of these questions is that they can be asked without impropriety and answered without embarrassment between complete strangers as well as intimates, yet provide, in a jiffy, deeply useful knowledge of the potential for relationship between us.

BIRTH STORIES

It is strangely true that what we remember being told about our births – or facts associated with our births – are precise metaphors for our relationships to other people. Since what we remember being told does not always correspond to the independent testimony of our parents, it seems we create our stories to match our achieved ways of experiencing others.

'I know nothing about my birth means, 'I have no understanding of how I relate to other people'. 'I/my mother nearly died' means, 'I/other people experience great distress in my relationships to them'. 'When she was pregnant with me, my mother could eat hardly any foods, but the few she could eat she loved' means, 'I don't like most people, but I have a few very loving relationships.'

A paranoiac schizophrenic told me, 'When I was born they held me upside-down and I cried and they laughed!'

NIRVANA AND SEX

For a new-born infant, in its inarticulate, undifferentiated self, the only experiences are total contentment or total pain. Thus the prototype for nirvana is the contentment of an infant at its mother's breast because its bliss is the reward for the absoluteness of its pain preceding the fulfillment of desire. The grown-up equivalent is the ecstasy of sexual orgasm with a partner whom we passionately love.

Sexual desire and its fulfillment is the most sought after experience because the arousal as well as the fulfillment is intensely pleasurable. This is due to the unique cooperation between the sympathetic and para-sympathetic nervous systems which sets sexual desire apart from all of the arousal and, in the right context, may be evaluated by us as the condition in life whose ecstasy rivals the fear of death in its intensity. This is the bonus of our creator's need for assurance that his creatures propagate.

LOVE AND NARCISSISM

While our sexual urges are so powerful that, in sufficiently restricted conditions, most of us would have sex with anybody of either sex or – dare it be said – even with animals, in normal circumstances we are instinctively highly selective in favour of narcissistic self-reflectiveness. But, in extremis, this tendency carries the risks associated with in-breeding so, notwithstanding the prevalence of incest amongst the morally degenerate, we are usually most powerfully attracted to others who are very, but not too much, like ourselves. First cousins often represent this ideal for each other.

Whether first cousins or not, isn't it amusing how often people obviously in love with each other are observably alike in colouring, overall body shape and size and especially, I notice, in idiosyncratic details of their physiognomy, from the overall shape of their faces to nose and mouth and ear shapes to rarely placed dimples and moles.

Narcissism rules, OK?

PROSTITUTION

Popular received wisdom decrees that men abusively exploit women in buying their services as prostitutes, but it is actually women who exploit men in this transaction. Not withstanding that prostitutes – male and female – are often exploited and abused by pimps they become involved with, in the simple exchange between female prostitutes and their male clients it is the women who abuse the men.

For normal men (as well as women) the pleasure of sexual intercourse is incomparably enhanced when combined with emotional intimacy and, even without emotional intimacy, greatly enhanced for both parties by their awareness of the pleasure they are giving the other. For whatever reason a man is unable to get the free sex which would naturally boost his self-esteem, in his compulsively needy encounter with a prostitute she deeply humiliates him through her clear communication that he gives her no pleasure and is only tolerated for his money.

TENDERNESS VERSUS PASSION

The quest for loving sexual intimacy is a central pursuit of our lives. We seek maximum, secure, guaranteed tenderness *and* maximum high octane erotic excitement. But there is a zero-sum relation between these aims.

Traditionally, both men and women have opted for long-term tenderness over fickle eroticism since we anticipate wanting love for many years after our sexual desire and desirability has significantly waned. Many have had their cake and eaten it through tenderly secure marriages *and* insecure, passionate erotic extra-marital liaisons. Some couples manage this arrangement well, but for most it is a dangerous mix, often resulting in the loss of marriage partners and lovers. However unrealistically, most of us want to be tenderly loved and passionately desired in one exclusive relationship.

Lately I have noticed a trend in which couples maximize their security and excitement in committed monogamy that abjures living together. Is this the best way?

FEMININITY, MASCULINITY, HUMANITY

'Doing' is the masculine principle in us all; 'being' is the feminine principle in us all. So, by and large, men feel themselves unready for love before they have achieved some worldly success; and, by and large, women feel themselves unready wholeheartedly to pursue careers until they have an established loving relationship with a man. In the long run, men need to be as well as do and women need to do as well as be in order to be wholesome human beings.

But it is in the development of spirituality through the quest for meaning in life that the doing and being principles and men and women transcend the attractions and antipathies of their oppositions and are reconciled in their common humanity.

Feeling and intuiting (Child) is the femininity in us all, thinking and knowing-how (Adult) the masculinity in us all, and believing (Parent) the humanity in us all.

LOVING

Being loving means willingly making other people feel good about themselves. It is giving thoughtful and genuine positive strokes. The best are Child to Child, which effectively say, 'You make me feel good' – which makes the other person feel good!

The more idiosyncratically pleasing a stroke is to the receiver, the more nourishing it is. So the better we know someone the more loving we can be to him or her. We know people through the answers they give to the questions we ask them. There is nothing more loving than asking questions.

Ritual good manners are the devices we are taught for behaving lovingly towards everybody even if we don't love them. There are stimuli that are usually understood to make the giving of a small positive stroke to another mandatory, such as saying please and thank you and excuse me a multitude of times in our mundane transactions.

MORALITY AND MOTIVE

In 2001, Harold Shipman a medical practitioner, was found guilty of murdering more than two hundred of his patients by injecting them with lethal doses of morphine. The ensuing enquiry concluded that "the motivation for his murders is incomprehensible *and* he is an incontrovertibly evil man". In the light of the first half of this judgement, I maintain that the truth of the second half cannot be vouchsafed.

A standard test of the moral maturity of a child is to pose a question like, 'Michael reaches in the cupboard for some sweet he is not supposed to eat and breaks a plate, knocking it off the shelf. Peter is helping his Mummy set the table for lunch. He accidentally trips and breaks three plates. Which boy is the naughtiest?' Children under the age of about eight answer Peter.

Sound moral judgments can only be made in the context of known intention.

MEASURING EVIL?

If the Yorkshire Ripper murdered twenty women and Harold Shipman murdered two hundred, is Shipman ten times more evil than the Yorkshire Ripper?

If we abjure such crude moral speciousness, and accept the relevance of intention in passing judgement, what intention did Shipman have in his multiple murders? Shipman has not declared his motive, so there are many plausible hypotheses we could surmise, but I guess, on the available facts, that he was seeking to rewrite his personal history.

When he was eighteen, Shipman witnessed his mother's agonizing death from cancer, from which trauma he admits he has never recovered. Every woman he painlessly murdered was a bid to make his mother die painlessly. Each murder failed in this aim, but he insanely tried again and again ...

If it were established that, in his addictive insanity, this was Shipman's aim, would this make his behaviour wholly good or partially evil or ... ?

GAMES

When life gives us pain it is intrinsic to our human nature to maintain our righteousness and blame others. We do this by playing 'games', which are set series of compulsive, ulterior transactions. There are three roles we adopt in playing games: Persecutor, Rescuer and Victim. All three roles are played by inauthentic parts of our Child ego state. We switch roles in the process of playing games but always end in the role consistent with our own righteous bad feelings. We unfailingly spot our complementary players across the most crowded room.

" 'Why don't you ... ?' 'Yes, but ... ' "is the most played game in the world.

Why-Don't-You starts as Rescuer of Yes-But as Victim, who pleads for help. In due course, Why-Don't-You confronts Yes-But with his resistance to following any suggestions offered. When Yes-But switches to Persecutor, accusing Why-Don't-You of being a terrible friend and Why-Don't-You ends up the unappreciated Victim.

PARENT VERSUS CHILD

Broadly speaking, the cultural influence of psychoanalysis prompts us to rationalize our neurotic propensities in terms of our imperfect relationships to our parents in childhood. Oldest children are inclined to perceive themselves as having been denied appropriate gratification of their (Child) feelings; youngest children are inclined to perceive themselves as having been denied appropriate gratification of their (Parent) desire to be respected; only children are inclined to perceive themselves as having been denied appropriate gratification of their feelings *and* their need for respect.

Consciously, as adults, we seek the kind of strokes we believe we were deprived of in childhood; but, unconsciously, the 'repetition compulsion' (made famous by Freud) ensures that we fail in this quest.

The inauthentic roles of Persecutor, Rescuer, the Victim and the devices by which we nominally seek strokes for our deprived ego state but succeed only in feeling bad about ourselves in old, familiar ways.

LOVINGNESS VERSUS
RIGHTEOUSNESS

Lovingness, which is based on our positive self-esteem, is the root of all goodness in us; righteousness, which is based on our fears about ourselves, ie our negative self-esteem, is the root of all evil in us.

In our relationships there is more or less continuous dialogue between the lovingness and righteousness in ourselves and the lovingness and righteousness in the other. When the lovingness in ourselves and another predominates over righteousness, love can be made and maintained; when the righteousness in ourselves and another predominates over lovingness, love will be killed or is already dead.

Our inauthentic righteousness is in need of constant reinforcement to maintain the very tenuous belief in our goodness that it gives us. 'I am holier than thou' is the belief we seek to protect ourselves from our fears. This is the antithesis of the equality which is the only medium in which love thrives.

TRANSSEXUALISM

In recent years it has become possible and permissible for many desperate people to be physiologically and anatomically (more or less) transformed from one sex into the other. They all avow that this is unrelated to their sexual orientation and refers only to their deep, lifelong knowledge that their anatomy is incompatible with their true gender. What is it that they know with such unassailable conviction and despair?

Whatever else transsexualism implies, it certainly puts paid to the, until recently, fashionable notion that observable differences of outlook, predispositions, and behaviour between the sexes are essentially conditioned rather than innate?

While most of us are lucky enough to have our gender awareness and our anatomies appropriately matched, the few who do not, bear incontrovertible witness to our bodies (usually) only representing our more profound, invisible gender. Where is gender located? In our brains? What makes living the wrong gender so unbearable?

Exodus

PERSONALITY TYPES

MORALITY AND MEANING

We never fully come to terms with the meaninglessness that death makes of our mundane concerns. Some people deny death by a belief in some form of eternal afterlife, others seek a symbolic continuation of their lives after physical death through being remembered for their works or deeds, and most of us find some comfort in the knowledge of the survival of some of our genes in our children, grandchildren, and further descendants. But, one way or another, contentment in the face of our mortality is contingent on our living life as if it has meaning, even if it doesn't.

We make sense and meaning of life by concepts and categories into which we sort our experiences. First and foremost we seek the meaning of pain. Universally, this quest creates in our minds the concept of 'good and evil' with its inevitable moral derivatives of blame and responsibility, righteousness and guilt.

SAMENESS AND DIFFERENCE

Categorizing is the primary function of our brains. People are piqued by being categorized because it discounts their exceptional characteristics in which most people take such pride. Nevertheless, the two most interesting observations that can be made about people are their samenesses and their differences. 'It's a girl' or 'It's a boy' is the fist observation ever made about any human being, and many other dichotomous characterizations by which we described people and the world derive from this basic category of gender.

How far we go in refining our categorization of a person depends on context. 'Man' is sufficient in the context of public lavatories; 'female, teenager, size 10' to a clothes manufacturer; 'intelligent, moderate socialist' for a trade union election. We know more about our friends, and want to know and describe a beloved down to the tiniest freckle of his or her physical and psychological being.

CATEGORIZING

Categorizing ourselves and others by constructs that are appropriately deep and comprehensive enlarges our awareness of the samenesses and differences between people. And, for the price of forgoing some of our narcissistic allegiance to our intrinsic uniqueness, we gain a corresponding diminishment of shame for our shortcomings, which we can now accept as 'only human'. Unless we categorize people, we implicitly assume all our own characteristics to be the human norm and we discount people who are unlike us.

Categorizing ourselves and others psychologically helps us to bring out the most and the best rather than the worst and the least in ourselves and others.
Understanding the dynamic meaning of our own type in relation to the known type of another individual enables us to please that individual with finesse, if we so desire, and most effectively defend our vulnerabilities again the assaults of that individual, if the need arises.

WE ARE ALL HOLOGRAMS

We are holograms. Given enough attention, any part of us can be seen to be representative of our wholeness. Palmistry, iridology, graphology, physiognomy, reflexology, astrological sun-signs, homeopathy, acupuncture, psychological typologies, blood groupings, phrenology, racial stereotyping, socio-economic groupings, national stereotypes, biochemistry, anatomical typing, kinaesthology, Enneagram types … all bear witness – some more successfully than others – to our instinctive appreciation of our holographic nature. All that is required is a prolonged, fascinated, obsessive concentration on some sign to evolve a coherent, holistic theory. A four foot six inch high dwarf who was also, briefly, something of a television celebrity, avowed that he had constructed a reliable personality typology out of his perception of the shapes of people's nostrils!

Body and mind and nature and nurture are inextricably entwined as the determinants of our achieved wholeness. But for each of us there is an essence which all our theories seek to isolate and understand.

FIVE BASIC TYPES

Out of my 28 years as a TA psychotherapist I have developed a theory of personality types and their interactions with each other that applies to nations as well as to individuals. There are five basic types: Be Perfect, Hurry Up, Please Me/You, Try Hard, and Be Strong. They are the ways in which our egos defend themselves against pain. To the extent that we are all human, they are each in all of us; to the extent that we are all different they are variously arranged hierarchically and combined in our personalities. Each type is clearly associated with one of more of the roles of Persecutor, Rescuer, and Victim.

Be Perfect plays the role of Persecutor.
Hurry Up plays the role of Victim.
Please Me/You plays all three roles of Persecutor,
    Rescuer, and Victim.
Try Hard plays the roles of Persecutor and Victim.
Be Strong plays the role of Rescuer.

BE PERFECT

Be Perfect is the defence against the fear of death. He/she is dominant over all other personality types and is supremely righteous – both morally and factually – in his/her bid to out-control God (or the powers that be).

Be Perfect is the one who always (or never) steps on the lines of the pavement and always waits for her train on exactly the same spot on the platform, and double-checks that the door is locked and all the gas taps off before she goes to bed. She is punctiliously reliable and dutiful. She is hypochondriac and is prone to high blood pressure. Her backlash is depressions. She *saves* and *makes* time and money.

Be Perfect is legitimized in organization and religious observance. Moderately expressed, it is the most honourable, constructive, healthy way to live. In extremis, it dives into the most hateful and destructive syndrome of bigotry, fanaticism and murderous rage.

HURRY UP

Hurry Up is the defence against the fear of life. He/she is the least adapted to the personality types and is supremely needy of others to control its self-destructive propensities.

Hurry Up is lively, spontaneous and active. She has a devil-may-care attitude to most things and is ready to do anything that promises immediate excitement. She is eager to form friendships and is extremely enthusiastic about any new person she meets who takes her fancy. But she is equally inclined to end any relationship hysterically and abruptly as soon as the other fails to provide her with unconditional love. She is invariably late and very accident-prone. Her backlash is alienation and futility. She *kills* time and *loses* money.

Hurry Up is legitimized in occupations involving speed, movement, and risk-taking. Moderately expressed, it is the most spirited, charming, and adventurous attitude to life. In extremis, it is mania or paranoia.

PLEASE ME/YOU

Please Me/You is the defence against the fear of responsibility. He/she is conventionally nice but sometimes very rude, obedient to win approval but also seeks to control others, through manipulation rather than overt dominance.

It is Please Me/You who helps blind men and old ladies across the road, contributes her bit to charity, sends all the people she knows birthday and Christmas cards, and is generally committed to doing the right thing. She enjoys socializing and dressing and furnishing her home in as stylishly fashionable ways as she can afford. She is inclined to digestive disorders. Her backlash is being misunderstood and blamed. She *fritters* time and money.

Please Me/You is legitimized in hierarchical organizations in which people are both bosses and bossed, and in occupations in which a uniform is *de rigeur*. Moderately expressed, it is the most civilized way to live. In extremis, it is shallow, smarmy inauthenticity.

TRY HARD

Try Hard is the defence against the fear of failure. He/she is both aggressive and humbly submissive, persistent against the odds or resignedly unambitious.

Try Hard is deeply sympathetic to the cause of the underdog. He is an ardent and tireless worker for the political party, usually left-wing, or any other cause that he believes in, and he uses acerbic wit to deflate the pompous and smug. But in his own interests, despite his competitiveness, he lacks confidence, is forever procrastinating, and rarely fulfils his potential. He is inclined to stress-related illnesses. His backlash is feeling an inferior failure. He *squanders* time and money.

Try Hard is legitimized in occupations requiring patient repetition or where servility and some authorized aggression are combined, such as in the army or police force. Moderately expressed, it is a bravely and unrelentingly determined way to live. In extremis, it is pugilistic, get-nowhere, resentful aggression.

BE STRONG

Be Strong is the defence against the fear of rejection. He/she is uninvolved, proudly self-sufficient, brave and stoical, and always considers others' needs above his own.

It is Be Strong who leads his men into battle, is marvellous in a crisis, gets on with things, goes for brisk walks and rises at 6am to go for an early morning swim every day of the year. He never whines or complains and may wear a moustache to keep his upper lip hidden, just in case, despite his best efforts, it should slacken. He keeps himself healthy but is inclined to circulatory diseases. His backlash is loneliness. He *uses* time and money.

Be Strong is legitimized in public service and in occupations that are on the receiving end of people's complaints. Moderately expressed, it is the most unselfish and sensitively considerate way to live. In extremis, it is cold, isolated autism.

COMPOUND PERSONALITY TYPES

The five personality types, Be Perfect, Hurry Up, Please Me/You, Try Hard, and Be Strong are the atoms of personality. They combine into ten pairs which are the molecules of personality. While the five atoms of personality may be thought of as irreducible, the ten molecules are the smallest entities that reflect the hard-wired duality of our minds.

My observations as a psychotherapist led me to the perception that while we probably all have all five atomic types in our natures, most people have two types phenomenally dominant in their personalities. And reflecting on this data led me to realize that each type has some quality in common with each of the other types and some quality of oppositeness to each of the other types.

In any individual's personality a given pair will thus contain an existential conflict (oppositeness) and the means to struggle effectively to resolve that conflict (sameness).

UNCOMMITTED DOUBTERS

Uncommitted Doubters (Be Perfect-Hurry Up) balance the most basic duality in us all, the fear of death and the quest for excitement. Manic-depression and alcoholism and drug-addiction are dis-eases of this type. Some normal signs of this personality are observable in individuals who alternate between thinking too long and too hard, and rashly rushing into things; or who are reliably unreliable to a precise degree, such as always being seven minutes late for appointments; or who want to belong and not belong at the same time, exemplified in people who are members of unusual religious or other communities.

The core dichotomy of this personality is safety or danger and the existential decision it represents is something like, 'I and the whole world are either mad or bad, but I'm not sure which.' When Uncommitted Doubters transform guilt into organization and panic into efficiency, they may become truly Passionate Philosophers.

RIGHTEOUS BLAMERS

Righteous Blamers (Be Perfect-Please Me/You) balance moral absolutism and moral relativism. They typically rise to power quickly in hierarchical organizations, being so capable of both giving and obeying orders and of manipulating other people as well as driving themselves very hard.

Child feelings and Parent beliefs are contaminated in this personality, which declares an incomplete resolution of attachment to the opposite-sexed parent, a common consequence of being spoilt by that parent and having a weak same-sexed parent.

The core dichotomy of this personality is control or be controlled and the existential decision it represents is something like, 'If I make the wrong decision I will be culpable and feel guilty, but so long as I make no choice I am being good, so nobody can blame me for what goes wrong.' When Righteous Blamers transform guilt into organization and feeling misunderstood into flexibility they may become truly Responsible Leaders.

FIGHTERS OF LOST CAUSES

Fighters of Lost Causes (Be Perfect-Try Hard) balance absolute and relative achievement. Fighters of Lost Causes are competitive and dominating, but also easily humiliated. They are found in occupations like music or sport where there is always room for improvement and success demands constant practice. They have not resolved their rivalry towards their same-sexed parent towards whom they feel timidly inferior and angry.

The core dichotomy of this personality is victory or defeat and the existential decision it represents is something like, 'Nobody attains my ideals and I'm not as good as I should be either. If I do bad things other people may excuse me, and then I am relieved, but I would feel more loved if they punished me and told me what I've done wrong.' When Fighters of Lost Causes transform guilt into organization and fear of failure into persistence they may become truly Committed Champions.

COLD INTELLECTUALS

Cold Intellectuals (Be Perfect-Be Strong) balance passionate rationality and cool empiricism. They demand the right to do things their own way, so are unlikely to be successful employees unless given lots of autonomy. Their emotional vulnerability prompts them to remain aloofly self-sufficient as far as is humanly possible. They are best suited to self-employment.

The core dichotomy of this personality is self-denial or being rejected, and the existential decision it represents is something like, 'Other people cannot cope with my needs as well as their own. Since their needs are greater than mine I have no right to ask for anything from them. So long as I need nothing from others I will not be tempted to ask for anything, and so I can remain blameless.' When Cold Intellectuals transform guilt into organization and feeling unappreciated into being resilient they may become truly Independent Thinkers

SORRY SINNERS

Sorry Sinners (Hurry Up – Please Me/You) balance adaptiveness and maladaptiveness in a sparklingly attractive but unreliable personality. Sorry Sinners begin relationships quickly and enthusiastically but can destroy them equally quickly through their hysterical and violent demandingness. They are volatilely unpredictable and both paranoically hostile and symbiotically clinging.

The core dichotomy of this personality is terrifying aloneness or suffocating conformity and the existential decision it represents is something like, 'I could love life if only I could find somebody to love me in the way I want to be loved, that is with unconditional love from their Parent to my Child. I try so hard to be good, and sometimes I think I am loved but then the other person always soon stops loving me and tells me to go to hell.' When Sorry Sinners transform panic into efficiency and feeling misunderstood into flexibility they become truly Lively Conformists.

ANGRY OUTSIDERS

Angry Outsiders (Hurry Up – Try Hard) balance feeling inferior failures with being alienated outsiders. In extremis, they are Hell's Angels and violent criminals. Less extremely, they are con men, militant trade-unionists, militant women's rights advocates … or militant anything. The passive version is the derelict of laid back drop-out. In general, Angry Outsiders are snarling, derisive and cynical. They hate 'the system' and all authority figures, and only work at all for the money they need for their personal, usually profligate, pleasures.

The core dichotomy of this personality is rage or futility and the existential decision it represents is something like, 'There's nothing you can do for me or give me and I'll punch you if you try. I'm no good but neither are you. The world is one big shit heap'. When Angry Outsiders transform panic into efficiency and fear of failure into persistence they may become truly Roving Adventurers.

FRIGHTENED LONERS

Frightened Loners (Hurry Up – Be Strong) are the most isolated of all the personality types. They balance terrified neediness with aloof self-sufficiency. They are very vulnerable to all kinds of self-destructive behaviour. Positively, they are courageous adventurers and heroes, such as solo yachtsmen, polar explorers and mountaineers. Women with this personality are often made briefly happy in becoming mothers whereby they are able to perceive the utter dependency of their infants as an expression of unconditional love given by their infants to them.

The core dichotomy of this personality is reject or be rejected and the existential decision it represents is something like, 'I can make no sense of people or the world. The world is strange and cold and I am lost in it. Anyone who loves me is a shit.' When Frightened Loners transform panic into efficiency and feeling unappreciated into resilience they may become Brave Individualists.

HUMBLE SERVANTS

Humble Servants (Please Me/You – Try Hard) balance conformity and self-esteem. They are stereotypically working class and respectable. Their personalities are timid, proper, conventional, know their place and do not question life as they find it. But they are not without pride and can be patronizing as well as servile. Knowing their own place implies the obligation for others to know their place too. Humble Servants are usually content to stay in lowly occupations that offer long-term security which they value above expectations of promotion and increased earnings. They gain self-esteem through association with their employer's status.

The core dichotomy of this personality is niceness or power and the existential decision it represents is something like, 'As long as people do as they are told no harm will come to them'. When Humble Servants transform feeling misunderstood into flexibility and fear of failure into persistence they may become truly Contented Workers.

DO-GOODERS

Do-Gooders (Please Me/You – Be Strong) balance emotional relatedness and self-sufficiency. They are courteous, considerate, nice but sometimes nasty; practical and helpful but also aloof, uptight, and secretly resentful of the impositions of others on their goodwill. It is the personality type most associated with helping professions like nursing, voluntary aid, and social work and any occupations where pleasant responsiveness to others' needs or demands is called for. Do-Gooders doubt their own loveworthiness and find it difficult to accept *strokes* for just being themselves; but they can more readily accept *strokes* if they feel they have *earned* them through unselfish giving to others.

The core dichotomy of this personality is control or vulnerability and the existential decision it represents is something like, 'I look after others when, by rights, they should be looking after me.' When Do-Gooders transform feeling misunderstood into flexibility and feeling unappreciated into resilience they may become truly Generous Carers.

PROUD LOSERS

Proud Losers (Try Hard – Be Strong) balance feeling inferior with aloof non-competitiveness. Proud Losers are often exploited by others because, though they may have much to offer, their self-conscious timidity prevents them declaring their ideas soon enough to be heard. So more self-confident rivals may steal their good ideas and get credit for them. Proud Losers typically dislike but endure their work, whatever it is. Because they are little noticed in their jobs they tend to withdraw into their private dreams.

The core dichotomy of this personality is frustration or resignation and the existential decision it represents is something like, 'The struggle to get what I want is not worthwhile because successful people never appreciate my worth, so I'd rather be with losers who I know are inferior to me'. When proud Losers transform fear of failure into persistence and feeling unappreciated into resilience they may become truly Quiet Achievers.

HANG-UPS AND TALENTS

Our hang-ups and our talents are two sides of one coin. It is the human drive to find positive meaning for our inhibitions and pains that, individually and collectively, has produced all the ideas and artefacts of civilization. I believe it is far from fortuitous that Beethoven was deaf, Monet blind, and Freud had cancer of the mouth. Without our uniquely human consciousness of self there would be no despair and no exultation. The trick is overcoming fear, which can only be done by doing what we most fear even while we are frightened.

As Shakespeare (who knew everything) put it in *Hamlet*:

> "Assume a virtue, if you have it not.
> … Refrain tonight;
> And that shall lend a kind of easiness
> To the next abstinence: the next more easy;
> For use almost can change the stamp of nature
> And master ev'n the devil or throw him out
> With wondrous potency."

CULTURAL PERSONALITY TYPES

Cultures, like individuals, have personalities. So, too, do domesticated animals, and pets are obviously chosen for the compatibility – by identification or complementarity – between them and their owners.

Climate is an influence on a nation's personality. The cold climates of northern Europe tend to induce Be Strong, the warmer climates of middle Europe tend to Please, and the very hot climates of southern Europe tend to Hurry Up. And any culture in which religion is a powerful background force is inevitably Be Perfect.

I am confident of these national stereotypes: the English are Be Strong-Please, the French overwhelmingly Be Perfect. The Italians are Be Perfect-Hurry Up, as are the Irish. America is Try Hard – Hurry Up, as is Australia. The Japanese are Please-Try Hard. The Israelis are Be Perfect-Please and the Palestinians Be Perfect-Try Hard.

Cats are Be Strong, dogs are Please, horses are Hurry Up.

PERSONALITY
INTERACTIONS

Although we all have all of the five personality types in
our basic human nature and so also have some,
however small, bits of each of the compound types, by
and large most individuals' personalities are dominated
by one compound pair that express their core existential
conflict and its bid for resolution. And in all of our
intimate relationships we instinctively choose others
whose personalities are like or complementary to our
own. Like to like is most often experienced as friendship;
complementary types are often chosen in love.

So in most intimate relationships two core personality
types in one person interact in four possible ways with the
two core personality types in the other. Some of these
interactions will be harmonious, some painful.
Knowledge of our own and others' typology can facilitate
us in choosing to interact with each other amongst our
happier options. There are fifteen possible interactions.

BE PERFECT AND BE PERFECT

Be Perfect and Be Perfect, like most couplings of like-to-like, usually get on well with each other. They are apt to be united in their common beliefs and values, and so long as they do not disagree fundamentally about what is and is not important in life, they give each other the security of feeling right about things. Their life together tends to be ritualistic, extremely well-organised and ordered.

Responsibilities are clearly articulated and divided between them, which they each fulfil dutifully and meticulously. Ideally, they tease each other out of excessive rigidity and intolerance. However, if they do disagree fundamentally about their values they will bicker and criticize each other interminably and probably end up feeling intransigent mutual hatred. A negative Be Perfect to Be Perfect relationship is epitomized in the internecine war in Northern Ireland, the Israel-Arab conflict, and in all religious wars that have ever been fought.

HURRY UP AND HURRY UP

Since the deep – however unconscious – intention of Hurry Up in relation to others is, 'I'll reject you before you can reject me', an intimate relationship between two people who are both principally Hurry Up is so unstable that it is unlikely to be formed at all. Phenomenally, though, each is obsessed with finding unconditional and lasting love. So when two Hurry Up's meet they often experience themselves as falling passionately in love at first sight, and tend to fall straight into bed with each other at their first meeting. The relationship usually ends a short time later when one of them simply doesn't turn up to an arranged meeting or in some way expresses as much hateful lack of regard for the other as he or she expressed loving commitment at their first meeting. As casual friends, they will tend to get drunk or 'stoned out of their minds' together.

PLEASE ME/YOU AND PLEASE ME/YOU

A couple who are both Please Me/You are usually united in a stable relationship of mutual dependence. Each of them is terrified of being left along, so they are both rigidly obedient to their unspoken agreement that they will behave towards each other in accordance with conventional propriety in general and in the ways each other ask in particular. Thus they achieve the emotional security they crave above all else. The price they pay is the stifling of spontaneity and authentic expression of emotion. Neither risks offending the other and so disturbing the safe equilibrium of the relationship, but to an outsider the suppressed resentment between them is often palpable. Sometimes this relationship continues on an even keel for a lifetime; sometimes the essential politeness of the relationship is punctuated with periodic angry quarrels which release the built-up resentment each feels for his or her symbiotic dependence on the other.

TRY HARD AND TRY HARD

Of all the like-to-like relationships between the personality types Try Hard and Try Hard is the one least likely to work for the benefit of both partners. (Hurry Up and Hurry Up is equally unbeneficial to both partners but rarely endures for more than a few months anyhow.) At best, Try Hard and Try Hard may be united in hostility and envy towards most other people who may, for example, find expression in their working together for a lost cause. However, more usually, the envious hostility of each is projected onto the intimate other, with each chronically criticizing the other in order to boost his or her own very precarious self-esteem. Each tends secretly to sabotage the other's achievement of his or her ambitions, and they are both constantly on tenderhooks lest the other win over them in some way. Life together for this couple is one long aggressive competition.

BE STRONG AND BE STRONG

The relationship between Be Strong and Be Strong is characterized by a great deal of mutual independence. Each is especially averse to what they would call emotional suffocation, so they support each other's need for regular periods of aloneness to pursue private interests or just meditate. They share the conviction that reliability is the better part of love. So long as both have important interests outside as well as within the relationship they get on very well together, and are grateful for their intimacy and commitment to each other which relieves them of the pain they each experienced as single people reaching out for love. If one of them does not have an important interest outside the relationship he or she will become resentful of the lack of time given to the relationship by the other; one will feel neglected and the other harassed.

BE PERFECT AND HURRY UP

At the profoundest levels of their personalities Be Perfect and Hurry up are supremely well matched because they are respectively the expressions of the fear of death and the temptation of death. To this extent Be Perfect is a cowardly stick-in-the-mud and Hurry Up is a brazen daredevil. They are able to cancel out the unhealthy extreme that each on its own stands for and to create instead an optimally healthy balance between organization and efficiency, thrift and extravagance, caution and daring, structure and spontaneity, right wing and left wing politics … and many other adaptive compromises between a wide range of polarities in life. Transactionally, Be Perfect tends to play the role of sometimes indulgent and sometimes controlling Parent to the sometimes charming and sometimes exasperating Child of Hurry Up. Only if they escalate their natures to a pathological degree can they harm each other by colliding in murderous/suicidal insanity.

BE PERFECT AND PLEASE
ME/YOU

The relationship between Be Perfect and Please Me/You is usually stable and contented, based on agreed dominance and submission roles. Be Perfect is the boss and Please Me/You is happily obedient. Be Perfect's quest for having things exactly the way (s)he wants is fulfilled and Please Me/You is profoundly reassured in knowing (s)he is doing the right and good thing. 'You have done well', given by Be perfect is usually received by Please Me/You as a positive stroke even though others might resent the patronage implied. However, because of their contented equilibrium, Be Perfect tends to lack any challenge to his rigidity and Please Me/You is not stretched to live outside her repressive conventionality. Sometimes Please Me/You episodically expresses some fleeting defiant rebelliousness and Be Perfect responds with angry criticism. But Perfect controls the outburst of Please Me/You and things usually return rapidly to their normal peace and calm.

BE PERFECT AND TRY HARD

The relationship between Be Perfect and Try Hard is an obviously unhappy one, based on open warfare. They are critical of each other but Be Perfect, who tends to be the more intelligent in this partnership is the one who consistently ends of being the victorious Persecutor while Try Hard ends up the humiliated Victim. Try Hard admires and envies Be Perfect's conviction of her rightness and Be Perfect disdains Try Hard. Be Perfect is using Try Hard to project her own feeling of worthlessness onto another while Try Hard is reinforced in his fundamental belief that 'No matter how hard I try, I'll never be successful enough.' Be Perfect often threatens to leave Try Hard but she secretly knows that she is dependent on Try Hard for her needed feeling of superiority. Both know their relationship is likely to continue in its often violent unhappiness for a long time.

BE PERFECT AND BE STRONG

When Be Perfect and Be Strong form a couple they are united by a puritanical attitude to life. They are both ambitious and work hard to achieve their goals. Be Perfect easily accommodates to Be Strong's view that reliability is the better part of love, and Be Strong pleases Be Perfect by being willing to get on with things dutifully without complaining. They are likely to enjoy conversations with each other that are serious, playfully critical, and ironical. They are unlikely to cause each other much pain although they tend to reinforce rather than modify each other's essential over-conscientiousness at the expense of Child spontaneity and pleasure. In their bossy righteousness they are very similar although Be Perfect is passionate where Be Strong is cool. To this extent Be Perfect may accuse Be Strong of being cold and Be Strong may accuse Be Perfect of being prejudicially overly involved.

HURRY UP AND PLEASE
ME/YOU

For Hurry Up, his or her relationship with Please Me/You is nearly as good as a relationship with Be Perfect. Although Be Perfect offers more of the control that Hurry Up so desperately needs, Please Me/You offers Hurry Up considerable reassurance. Hurry Up says, 'It's no good expecting love to last. People give it to you for a little while then they inevitably abandon you.' To which Please Me/You replies, 'I know how you feel, how frightening it is to think of being left alone. But it's not inevitable. So long as you are good the people who love you will stay with you forever. Let me show you how to be good.' Through this implicit dialogue Hurry Up learns social adaptiveness and his terror is diminished; and Please Me/You gains the reassurance of security she gets from knowing her partner's emotional dependence on their relationship is even greater than her own.

HURRY UP AND TRY HARD

The relationship between Hurry Up and Try Hard is full of tension and aggression. Try Hard is driven crazy by Hurry Up and Hurry Up is made wildly impatient by Try Hard. Hurry Up needs a self-confidently controlling other, but Try Hard can only manage the aggression of *un*-self-confidence. And Hurry Up, being completely absorbed in her own neediness, is incapable of giving Try Hard the "tough love" he needs to overcome his inferiority complex. Each justifies his or her inadequacies in terms of the provocation of the other. Hurry Up says, 'If he weren't so damn slow I could be calm.' Try Hard says, 'If only she'd give me some peace I could fulfil my ambitions and my potential.' Neither of them achieves anything positive by this dishonest projection of responsibility for their hang-ups but they may eventually succeed in provoking violence or serious bodily illness in each other.

HURRY UP AND BE STRONG

The most painful relationship of all is the one between Hurry Up and Be Strong. Each is convinced of the inevitability of profound loneliness, and they powerfully support each other's affirmation of this conviction. The relationship usually begins with Be strong as Rescuer of Hurry Up as Victim, but Hurry Up quickly begins persecuting Be Strong who then becomes the Victim. Hurry Up proves that love offered is not enough and doesn't last anyway and Be Strong proves that what he has to offer is unappreciated, therefore he must be unworthy of love. That these two choose to form a relationship with each other at all bears witness to the sad truth that they are both unused to receiving love that they would be unable to cope with a relationship that offered it. Hurry Up asks for everything and gets nothing; Be Strong asks for nothing and gets nothing.

PLEASE ME/YOU AND TRY HARD

The relationship between Please Me/You and Try Hard is likely to be an amicable but dreary one. That is, neither is likely to hurt the other but neither will they stimulate each other to reach beyond the narrowly unambitious and respectable limits they impose on their lives. They 'know their place and accept it. In England it is a proto-typically lower-middle-class marriage in which the wife is the Please Me/You and the husband the Try Hard partner. Please Me/You is nice to Try Hard in not pressing him to achieve anything, and Try Hard confirms in his behaviour to Please Me/You's need to be respectable. The worst they are likely to do to each other from time to time is for Try Hard to think, but rarely say aloud, that Please Me/You is affected and pretentious, and for Please Me/You to think, but rarely say aloud, that Try Hard is a failure.

PLEASE ME/YOU AND BE STRONG

The relationship between Please Me/You and Be Strong is basically an unhappy one, but one which often endures for a lifetime. It is frequently the chief component of English middle-class marriages, the husband being the Be Strong and the wife the Please Me/You partner. The trouble is that the relationship offers each of them easy affirmation of their most painful feelings without providing any positive compensations. Please Me/You is dependent on another's instructions as to how to behave to please the other person; Be Strong longs to have his needs understood and met without his having to give voice to them. Please Me/You asks Be Strong to tell her what to be and to do; Be Strong replies, 'I want you to give to me in a spontaneous and authentic way, not according to instructions.' Thus Please Me/You feels misunderstood and falsely vilified; and Be Strong feels unappreciated and unloved.

TRY HARD AND BE STRONG

Try Hard and Be Strong are incompatible types who are essentially incapable of gratifying each other, so a lasting relationship between them is unlikely. Try Hard aims for what she wants materially in such a way as not to achieve it; Be Strong asks for what he wants emotionally in such a way as not to get it. They are on different wavelengths. Try Hard is competitively aggressive toward Be Strong, and Be Strong adopts a stance of cold and bored aloofness toward Try Hard. Try Hard envies Be Strong his cool control which Try Hard perceives herself as lacking because of insufficient luck of opportunity; and Be Strong finds Try Hard a bore for whining and generally wearing her heart on her sleeve. In transacting with each other Be Strong generally limits himself to peremptory brush-offs to Try Hard and Try Hard is consumed with frustration and rage.

PERCHANCE TO DREAM

In the past fifty years, since the discovery of Rapid Eye Movement connected with dreaming, research has revealed many complexities associated with that third of our lives we spend in sleep.

It is now known that REM sleep is associated with de-activating unresolved emotional arousal; and REM deprivation produces increasing agitation. Conversely, deprivation of non-REM sleep is associated with increasing depression.

I propose that REM and non-REM sleep are part of the homeostatic equilibrium we constantly seek, physiologically and psychologically, between Be Perfect and Hurry Up. REM sleep keeps Hurry Up in check and non-REM sleep keeps Be Perfect in check.

Barbiturates have long been prescribed for insomnia, but they reduce dreaming, so the price paid for a good night's sleep is increased waking irritability. But depressed people have relatively too much dreaming sleep and too little non-REM sleep; so perhaps barbiturates should be the first drug prescribed for depression.

Leviticus

FAITH

MEANING OF LIFE?

'Religion' is derived from the Latin word 'ligare' meaning to connect. 'Religare' means to reconnect ourselves to what underlies existence. That is man? What is the universe? How are the two related? Spirituality is our consciousness of these questions and desire to ponder them. Religions are our maps of the territory.

We are inside the universe as a given part of it and, by definition, the part cannot understand the whole. The goodness of religion consists of our submission to this truth; the multitudinous wars committed in the name of religion are affronts to this truth.

We want life to have meaning, but it may not; notwithstanding which we live our lives most contentedly when we act as if it has meaning even if it doesn't. Judaism's special wisdom is its disavowal of the need for belief, only right action being devotionally required. Religious rituals and ceremonies codify right action.

FEAR OF GOOD

To the vast majority of the world's illiterate or semi-literate masses religion is the only distraction from their daily imperative of finding enough to eat. Religion keeps them righteous, despite their misery, for fear of God's retribution, and compensates their misery with the hope of reward at least in the world to come. It is the concrete emotionally-bound relationship of a young child to its autocratic parent.

God existed for (or was invented by) our most remotely prehistoric ancestors. Even at our most primitive, religion and art are the *sine qua non* of our quest for meaning, which distinguishes us from all other species. Even at his most fearful, God is much better than Nothing.

Only the very few people on earth who have time for baroque worries and symbolic thought can afford the luxury of a Parent to Parent relationship to God, questioning his authority and even his existence.

MEANINGLESSNESS AND MYSTICISM

There may be no meaning of life. Espousing this possibility as a certainty eliminates the need to make sense of pain. Pain becomes merely one of the contingent facts of life in an arbitrary universe. Everything is simply the way it is and neither good nor bad, so we are wasting our time asking why. Non-reflective playing out of our lives in keeping with the biological propellants of our constitutions is all. This is the way of life for other species; and paradoxically this is also the position of the mystic, whose achieved attitude is of joyously interpreting everything we experience as "for no reason", just the way it is.

The way of the mystic is called transcendental, but the same way, when we refer to other species is not. This is so because mystics have transcended their fear of death; animals don't have a fear of death to transcend.

GOD, PAIN, AND DEATH

Whether or not God exists, we were bound to have invented Him to reassure ourselves that pain and death – which are our lot - have meaning and value beyond our immediate understanding and 'everything will be all right in the end'. While grown-ups are entitled to be atheists, agnostics, cynical nihilists … or anything else that makes God redundant, we have a duty to give our children an optimistic attitude to life and, once they know about death, this means giving them the benevolent omniscience and omnipotence of God.

God, with a long white beard sitting on a throne in the sky, is an enormously comforting reality to a child – a super-duper parent who goes on looking after us even when, *in extremis*, our own mortal parents do not. A child can always renounce God later but, when young, profoundly needs Him to make her existence and the universe complete and good.

FAITH

Our lives are full of quotidian, transitory pains as well as the continuous biggest pain, the knowledge of our mortality.

Because we know that we only seek pleasure, we judge our experienced pains as uncalled for and inexplicable, so unless we have *faith* that meaning is contained in our pains (even though we don't presently know that meaning) we will translate our feeling that we are experiencing something senseless into a bitter and nihilistic attitude to life itself. Thus, faith that there is a wisdom greater than our own in God (or the powers-that-be) is needed for us to interpret our pains as having a (presently unknown) *purpose* that is furthering our long-term happiness. We confirm this truth when we retrospectively interpret our past pains as having brought us knowledge without which we would be unable fully to appreciate our present joys and achieved sense of meaning in life.

FATE AND FREE-WILL

The problem of free-will has always been available for the pleasure of mental masochists. It cannot be solved, only dis-solved.

By definition, the human brain is only capable of comprehending that which is less complex than itself; and, by definition, our concept of fate refers to meaning more complex than we can apprehend, emanating as it does from a source those power is greater than our own. We can only dissolve the problem pragmatically by living at the highest level of free-will available to us while accepting, from the evidence, that there are bound to be times in our lives when a higher consciousness than we are capable of seems to mock our lower level morality and purpose.

Maybe, as Jung put it, "Free-will is doing that which I must, gladly." Or, as an unknown rabbi put it, "We've got to believe in free-will, we've got no choice."

THE NECESSITY OF CHOICE

Our free-will is contained in the responses we make to our fate. Our responses are our choices and we cannot avoid choosing. Passivity is the self-delusion of no-choice but of course it is a choice and, like all others, has consequences.

Every choice we make is the cause of the inexorable train of events that follows in its wake, to the natural conclusion of a happening in our lives. When a happening is painful we are loath to remember the moment of choice that determined it, although often our admission of responsibility is implicit in our obsessive fear of the concluding pain – too late – and a conscious struggle to avoid it. In our most intense moments we do know (in our hearts) the awful, simple truth that in virtually – if not absolutely – everything that befalls us we get exactly what we set out to get, and so what we deserve.

IS GOD GOOD?

In the few occurrences in our lives where even our unconscious motives are insufficient to account for what befalls us, we are reduced to impotent acquiescence to Fate – that is, God's Will. All that is left for us to decide is whether, on balance, God (and the universe) are benevolent or malevolent.

Be Perfect is the – ultimately trusting – religious view of life; Hurry Up is the – ultimately paranoic – futile view of life. Be Perfect keeps life ordered and safe but we need some Hurry Up to release us from the fearful, rigid stultification that Be Perfect can induce, and to allow ourselves some daring and exciting adventures. There is no love without hate, no good without evil. We are hard-wired for duality and the continuous homeostatic quest to find the right balance between opposites. Our overall contentment is contingent on our embracing somewhat more Be Perfect than Hurry Up.

FATE AND CREATIVE STRUGGLE

Much of our fate is equatable with the potential and limits of our genetic inheritance. We are free to respond with: impotent, angry frustration; placid, unambitious acceptance; or creative struggle. These correspond to: being five feet tall and wanting only to be an Olympic high jumper; having a beautiful voice and being content to sing only for oneself and the pleasure of a few friends; and, in whatever realm of our being and doing, stretching ourselves to the very limits of our capacity or endurance to reconcile desire with reality in achieving the nearly, but not quite, impossible.

The third option, creative struggle, along gives meaning and purpose to our lives, and can prevail from the largest to the smallest moments in our lives, from painting the ceiling of the Sistine Chapel to adding a cup of water to a pot of soup to cater for an unexpected guest.

IS GOD FAIR?

Concerning the unfairness of our fates, we are to God as insects are to us.

An insect being crushed under the will of my foot may simply and passively submit to its fate. Self-punitively, it may blame itself for not seeing my foot and avoiding it. Or, questioningly, it may ask why I chose to crush it. For the sin it committed against me by stinging me? (But think of all the insects who sting people and get away with it.) Maybe it didn't sting me and didn't even try, so rages against me for my injustice. Or did I crush it punitively in accordance with a morality beyond its ken? From a superior position, in order to humble it? Because I am evil?

It – and we – can never know unless all manifestations of the original Will are reabsorbed into it – which is the mystic's question and the Messianic promise.

THE GAME GOD PLAYS

If goodness was never rewarded and badness was never punished we would happily become moral nihilists. If goodness was always rewarded and badness always punished, we would have no need of moral debate. But the reality in which we live is that goodness is *usually* rewarded and badness *usually* punished.

We do avoid the pain of being burnt by being good and not touching hot stoves; but a completely unpredicted gas explosion may set fire to our house and us. We avoid being arrested and sent to gaol by being good and law-abiding; but Nazis can come and round us up and throw us into concentration camps. Love given is usually reciprocated; but sometimes love is responded to with a spit in the eye. Thus, by intermittent reinforcement – the most powerful of all conditioning techniques – God teases and tantalizes us into forever questing to understand His will.

FUNDAMENTALISM

God is what is left after the universe has been explained by the science of any age. Fundamentalism is the bid to make God a fact, like scientific knowledge. Its literalism misses the point that there cannot be just one true interpretation of anything. Kant demonstrated the inescapably solipsistic nature of our ideas, the impossibility of objectively matching our ideas to reality. The mystery of meaning is inviolate; there is no literal truth; subjectivity rules the universe.

Out of its adherents' desperate terror of death, fundamentalism avows the absolute one and only truth with absolute certainty of eternal life through privileged absolute knowledge of God. Unavoidably, it must righteously murder all infidels, whose mere existence threatens its precariously teetering security.

Fundamentalism is the goodness of Be Perfect escalated to insanity and evil. The healthy alternative is the ego-transcending playful laughter at the incomprehensible, absurd, but wonderful privilege of existence.

GOD VERSUS SCIENCE

The fight between God and scientific materialism lasted about 500 years. During this time God's omnipotence and omniscience were insulted, as faith was replaced by knowledge. At first God fought back valiantly, bringing down his wrath on hubristic man in the form of the Black Death and sundry other collective calamities, and on particular men and women in the form of inquisitions, burnings, and derision. But by the beginning of the twentieth century the theories of science could confidently account for the most horrendous acts of God in materialistic terms. To many more people than ever before God was toppled and presumed dead.

But our willingness to renounce God rested on the reassuring certainty of science which, in the course of the twentieth century was itself assaulted by Heisenberg's uncertainty principle, Einstein's theory of relativity, and the nihilistic horrors of black holes and chaos theory. We are left trembling at Nothing.

GOD AND US

To the theist, Man is made in God's image, to the atheist, God is made in Man's image. Either way God and Man are very alike. Notwithstanding our theologians' insistence that God is transcendent and unimaginable, to the child in us all He is an autocratic but benevolent super-duper omniscient, omnipotent parent.

The greatest humiliations of God were by Copernicus and Darwin who told us we are not at the centre of the universe and are not special among species. Freud capped it by telling us we don't even know our own minds. God, in our image, was likewise reduced to puny impotence.

We are presently struggling to outstare the emptiness of the godless universe. Now we have no choice but to fully de-anthropomorphize God in order to reinstate his superhuman awfulness and power, by which means we may hope that all religions will be reunited in Godly tolerance and peace.

NIHILISM

Notwithstanding the perils of fundamentalism, there is also peril in nihilism. Absoluteness unites them. The quest for meaning is at least implicit in every human being and we give ourselves meaning through formality and ritual which, when associated with an admittedly tenuous religious belief, gives us consolation for the inevitability of death and a sense of goodness in living life.

Religion pays homage to the magical thinking in all of us, which is based on our deep appreciation of the connectedness of the macro- and the micro-worlds. Negatively it is superstition, which fears the badness of the universe; positively it is prayer, which is not as is commonly supposed an appeal to God to make everything better, but the way in which we avow our agreement with God that everything is as it must and should be. We pray for rain in the rainy season, for harvests in summer.

THE DEATH OF GOD

People who now regularly attend churches, synagogues and mosques are mostly middle-aged or old. And for most of them it is no longer to worship a fully believed-in God but rather for the 'feel good factor' of belonging and the security of familiar rituals. Most young Christians, Jews and Muslims do not resonate to these rituals, and generally attend places of worship with their elders only under sufferance. But what young people do resonate to – probably more than their elders – is the new yearning in the world for spiritual meaning in our lives.

Many, especially young, people find less than satisfactory solutions to their spiritual quest in a paradoxical escalation of Be Perfect into rigid forms of fundamentalist Christian, Jewish or Muslim orthodoxy, or by defecting into equally pathological cults of one kind or another.

Atheism and fundamentalism are opposites that are identical in their expression of contemporary spiritual dis-ease.

RELIGION AND FEMINISM

In principle, religion is the spirituality that unites men and women in the mythical reunification of oppositeness that divides them. In practice, religious observance is a manifestation of the receptive, feminine being-ness in us all that opposes the active, masculine doing-ness in us all.

Men, born out of women's wombs, have a hard time finding the balance between asserting their separateness from women and acknowledging their dependence on them. Traditionally, the officers of religion – rabbis, priests and mullahs – have been exclusively male, a wise way of feminizing men while investing them with a sense of their masculine superiority. Latter-day feminism that insists on women's rights to hold religious office is a stupid disturber of the peace. Strong female wisdom allows men their little pompous exclusive authority which keeps them contentedly tame.

Few red-blooded men now choose a religious vocation, and churches are left with a closet full of homosexual priests.

RETURN TO POLYTHEISM?

It is part of the presumptuous pride of contemporary humanity that monotheism, represents huge evolutionary progress in humanity's consciousness and belief.

At the height of the Israeli-Palestinian conflict and fundamentalist religious belligerence elsewhere, Jasper Griffin in *The Spectator* (April 2002) with emperor's-new-clothes simplicity, asked if monotheism is, in fact, a degradation of polytheism and its intolerance and invocations of righteous pugnacity.

Monotheism's first commandment, "Thou shalt have no other gods before me" is a statement of exclusivity and intolerance. Is there not something a lot more civilized in polytheistic religions that allow their own and others' gods (and people) respectfully to co-exist? As Jasper Griffin put it, "There was ... something to be said for pagan days, when a new god could be signed up and expected to fit in with all the rest in a spirit rather like that in which a soccer club transfers a star player from another team."

ORTHODOXY AND HERESY

As for all doctrines, the sterility of religious orthodoxies has been a cyclically recurring phenomenon throughout history. Be Perfect and Hurry Up are in continuous dynamic tension individually and collectively. All beliefs begin as Hurry Up heresies and end as ossified Be Perfect forms. Rejuvenation is achieved by a new heresy that reconnects us with the ideal that presently meaningless ritual once enshrined.

Moderately expressed, all orthodoxies, in their conservatism, help us to feel safe while comfortably tolerating some dissent. Moderately expressed, all heresies, in their creativity, pay homage to the value of the orthodoxies they are injecting with a flammable spark.

But when the harmonious dialectic between orthodoxy and heresy breaks down, mutual appreciation is transmuted into an escalating battle for supremacy. Thus the inherent goodness in each metamorphizes into evil and, escalated to their highest pitches, their oppositeness collide in unitary insanity where murder and suicide become indistinguishable.

Numbers

THE ISSUE OF
ASTROLOGY

THE LIMITS OF THEORIES

In the collective human mind, theories about everything arise, have their day, and are discarded as newly observed facts force us to supersede them with theories that will accommodate the new facts as well as the old.

Nevertheless, 'there is nothing new under the sun' and those people we call original thinkers usually utter old truths in a new voice which is better attuned to the tone of their time. Copernicus revived the Greek idea of a sun-centred universe; Darwinian evolutionary theory had been espoused by various others since before the common era; the Unconscious had its place in literature long before Freud; and the ideas expressed by Ovid two and a half thousand years ago are as popular in the replies to the lovelorn in today's magazines as they ever were. Apples falling on people's heads and causing uniquely revelationary moments in human thought are a romantic myth.

MY MIND BOMB

I had been a psychoanalytically-oriented psychotherapist for several years when, one day in 1978, a man who had been in one of my therapy groups for two years asked me to listen to a tape-recording of a consultation he had just had with an astrologer. Indulgently, I agreed and listened to it with half an ear while attending also to the late afternoon cacophony of my children and their demands.

Within five minutes I was astounded. With no knowledge of my patient other than his time, place and date of birth the astrologer had already said everything – and more – about him that I had discovered in two years in laborious analysis. I consulted the same astrologer for myself and was overwhelmed by the authenticity and depth of what he told me. From then, my life has been transformed.

I offer the following essays to all my skeptical but open-minded readers.

ASTROLOGY AND HOLISM

The origins of astrology are lost in antiquity, but there seems to have been no country or early form of civilized community where astrology was not developed. The date of the first individual horoscope is unknown, but certainly by Greek times it had reach recognizable form, and Hippocrates maintained that no doctor was qualified if he could not interpret a patient's horoscope. For primitive man – and indeed for modern man up until at most five hundred years ago – nothing was inanimate. The validity of astrology was never questioned since it was completely consistent with every human being's acceptance of himself and his life as participating in the life of nature as a whole. Far from being blasphemous, astrology is the religious outlook on life, and its rejection by modern man runs entirely parallel to the general secularization of life in the Western cultures with which we are familiar.

THE ALGEBRA OF
EXISTENCE

The primary assumption of astrology is that anything that comes into existence – animate or inanimate, tangible or abstract – contains within itself, for all of its existence, the qualities of the moment it comes into being. And the qualities of that moment are contained in the map of the heavens at that moment as seen from that place, which map is read by astrologers.

A human being, an accident, a business, an earthquake, an idea that all come into being on the same date and at the same time and place will have identical horoscopes, but the astrologer will give these entities appropriately different readings. That is, a horoscope is like an algebraic equation with as many solutions as there are entities it represents.

The most popular use of astrology is in the interpretation of horoscopes applied to human beings, whose coming into existence is taken to be their first breath.

FATALISM AND PROPHECY

For the past 24 years astrology has illuminated my life. I am convinced of its validity by the evidence of my own life, the lives of people I know well, and by the feedback I get from my many astrological clients.

Yet only a very small proportion of intelligent and educated people are open to testing the tenets of astrology through their own experience. Those who reject astrology out of hand can be divided into two groups: the irreligious who fearfully dismiss it because they presume it to be fatalistic and thus a denial of their precious free-will; and the religious who angrily dismiss it as evil and blasphemous in its prophetic aspects. Both these justifications for turning away from astrology are specious and based on closed-minded ignorance.

The fatalism of astrology is no more than genetics; prophecy no more than the natural extension of the present into the future.

DESTINY AND FREEDOM

Astrology, seen as God's manifestation of His will, transcends our human dualistic notions of good and bad. Everything is simply the way it has to be. We are each dealt a hand of cards; God holds the pack. But most people live by the mutually contradictory beliefs that they choose freely, moment by moment, to play any card they like from the whole pack and that when they lose tricks it is due to other people holding better cards. In truth, no hand is intrinsically better or worse than any other; playing out a grand slam with a fistful of court cards and trumps can be as boring as playing an adroitly skilful game with no trumps or court cards can be joyful. As Martin Buber puts it in *I and Thou*, "Destiny confronts man as the counterpart of his freedom. It is not his boundary, but his fulfillment."

ASTROLOGY AND BIGOTRY

Astrology as a whole is attacked by the smugly ignorant high-IQ bigot on two grounds: that the precession of the equinoxes invalidates the astrological signs; and that the world cannot be meaningfully divided into twelve signs.

The precession of the equinoxes (which astrologers know all about) is irrelevant to Western astrology which is *not* based on the popularly named clusters of stars, but on an abstract division of the ecliptic, with zero degrees Aries beginning, by definition, at the spring equinox.

Concerning the sun-signs of popular astrology columns, dividing the world into twelve is a general but not useless division. (In the context of public lavatories, dividing the world into two categories is both useful and sufficient!) Daily sun-sign forecasts are valid but as general as a weather forecast which might say, 'Tomorrow will be hot and sunny. Dark-skinned people will be in their element, light-skinned people should stay indoors.'

ASTROLOGY PLUS SCIENCE

Astrology has been marginalized since the ascendancy of atomistic materialism from about the eighteenth century to the present day. But materialistic physics has had its day. In the wake of Heisenberg's Uncertainty Principle, the nihilistic horrors of Black Holes and Chaos theory, establishment science now espouses the doctrine of the certainty of uncertainty and, ironically, the communications of the most widely acclaimed scientists sound more and more like the most arcane speculations of academic philosophers and mystics.

The theme that is most likely to provide the link that will reconcile astrology and modern science is the concept of synchronicity, the idea first espoused by Jung, of acausal connectedness between happenings that, from the point of view of our rational conscious minds, are inexplicable. Astrology and Science seem about to shake hands over the "new" truth that the objective universe is inextricably interwoven with the subjectivity of the minds observing it.

ASTROLOGY PLUS PHYSICS

Ironically, physics is now more compatible with astrology that it was in Newton's time, although Newton was an astrologer.

The physical premise of astrology, that forces are transmitted without attenuation with increased distance and do not vary with respect to the differences of masses of the planets from which they originate, is inconsistent with Newtonian mechanics; but it is completely in accord with Einstein's photo-electric theory, which demonstrates that the effect of a photon does not diminish with distance. And modern chemistry and biology emphatically describe the properties of substances in terms of architectural configurations of the atoms within molecules, which is also analogous to astrological thought.

Dr Percy Seymour, Principal Lecturer in Astronomy at Plymouth University hypothesizes convincingly that the truth of astrology is explicable in terms of magnetic fields to which our nervous systems resonate, from our conception onwards. We are born when the cosmos plays our tune.

ASTROLOGY AND RELIGION

Contrary to much popular misapprehension astrology is not 'believed in' any more than a telephone is. Both are used because they work. All astrologically based choices and decisions are no more than extension of sailing with the tide, planting by the seasons, and forecasting rain from the configurations of the clouds, all of which bear witness to our ordinary, knowledgeable 'belief in' the connections between extra-terrestrial events and events on earth.

What might partly account for the popular assumption that astrology is a kind of pagan religion is that the realization of its empirical truth inevitably leads to a profound but non-specific religious orientation to life. That is, if we define all religiosity as a quest to understand our relationship to the cosmos (or God), then astrology is the most religious orientation to life there is, irrespective of the beliefs or unbeliefs of its practitioners. Einstein called himself a deeply religious unbeliever.

ASTROLOGY AS LANGUAGE

As a language, what makes astrology special is its deep and comprehensive understanding of the interconnectedness of things and events and its knowledge of equivalences beyond the capacity of any other language to encompass.

Nothing but astrology can see the equivalence of gas leaks, a sea-voyage, film-making, alcoholism, and mystical transcendence; of underground explosions, survival, obsessiveness, demagoguery, and psychological transformation; of electricity, independence, intuition, homosexuality, computing, and democracy; of bones, concrete, fear, self-discipline, endurance, and old-age; of obesity, good investments, long-distance travel, lawyers, publishers, and religion; of red blood cells, iron, sexuality, and accidents; of jewellery, sociability, justice, lust and good taste; of reasoning, nervousness, telephones, and versatility; of feelings, childhood, gynaecology, and changeability; of ambition, pride, masculinity, and the heart.

From the symbolic meanings of the sun, moon and planets, qualified by their configurations with each other and their zodiacal placements, the singularity of the universe can be apprehended.

ASTROLOGY AND GENETICS

No sane person doubts that we are unavoidably constrained by our genetically determined physicality in the colour of our eyes, our gender, our blood group, and the many programmes which determine, for example, our acquisition of teeth, the onset of puberty, and the greying of our hair. Despite the environmental conditions which – especially in the formative years of childhood – may modify our genetic programming, by and large we accept that there are actually very narrow limits to the power of external influences. No more and no less is implied in the determinism of astrology.

The wondrous joy we experience at a birth is in the unactualized *potential* contained in a new human being. What will her inheritance enable her to do and to be? What can she – and we – do to fulfil rather than frustrate her desires within the bounds of the assets and liabilities of her pre-determined nature?

POTENTIALITY AND CONTINGENCY

The knowledge of a person that can be derived from her horoscope is deep and comprehensive. But the language of the horoscope is symbolic, and the quality of any interpretation of it is so dependent on both the skill and artistry of the interpreter that it is extremely difficult to objectify the information. The best astrologers can only suggest the ways in which the configurations of the horoscope are most likely to be manifest in the life of a person it describes.

As for our genetically determined characteristics, who can say that a tall and athletic man will choose to use these endowments to be a basketball player or a high-jumper, a nightclub bouncer, a mugger, or a policeman … or not both to use these attributes at all? But once we know he is a basketball player we can readily see his characteristics that enabled him to become one.

POTENTIALITY AND
FULFILLMENT

Life is full of alternatives within the constraints of
determinism, and potentiality does not guarantee
actuality. Consulting a railway timetable does not imply
the necessity of catching or missing a train. Acorns may
grow into oak trees; some do, some don't. Astrologically
speaking, some Neptune configurations suggest a
vulnerability to alcoholism and/or spirituality. A whisky
priest may be a hopeless drunk *and* a truly devout man.
Some Mars configurations suggesting bloodshed may
manifest equally plausibly in a butcher, surgeon, or
murderer.

Furthermore, everyday language is imbued with value-
judgements. Who decides when courage is foolhardiness
or valiant altruism? when ambition is aggressive
selfishness or worthy pursuit of goals? when love is
clinging dependency or loyalty?

All of this understanding is now articulated in leading
edge genetic theory, as it always has been in astrology
which is profoundly aware of the interaction of
potentiality and contingency and whose symbols are
value-free.

FINAL CAUSE?

Physically and psychologically our completed selves are products of nature and nurture. Nurture has its say – witness the increased height of recent generations and our increased longevity due to improved nutrition and hygiene – but nature is dominant and is precisely mapped in our horoscopes as well as our genes.

Our remembered childhood experiences, which our literary tradition and latterly, psychoanalysis call causes of our completed selves are actually selectively remembered by us to concur with our preordained genetic predispositions. Witness the often widely divergent memories and/or interpretations of shared experiences of siblings.

But it doesn't matter that the environmental events of our early years are not really causes, but are subsumed to the deeper determinism of our genes which, in turn, may be subsumed to an even deeper cause, to karma, astrology … or whatever, until we stop and call the "final cause" God – or Unified Field Theory or what you will.

PREDICTION AND PROPHECY

We make (short-term) predictions and (longer-term) prophecies every time we use the future tense. Nearing home after a family outing, the child says, 'Rover will be pleased to see us'. Planning a dinner party we say, 'We must invite David and Susan to meet each other. They'll get on famously.'

Our predictions are sometimes mistaken but often realized. Short-term predictions generally have best chances of success because of the relatively few unexpected events that can intervene between now and then. Every instant of 'now' is the necessary consequence and culmination of every previous moment in history, but was only a probability – however great – before it occurred. And nothing that has already happened could have been otherwise.

Our uncertainties keep us hopefully on our toes. Market research has revealed that the two most often cited reasons people give for reading newspapers are for the weather forecast and their horoscopes.

THE COURAGE OF PROPHETS

The courage of prophets is their willingness to know and announce the outcome of present trends while still being bound to the necessity of continuing along the path already chosen to its conclusion.

Astrology is the algebra of human consciousness. Mundane subject-matters are the arithmetic of life, and for the astrologer's prophecies to be most reliable (s)he needs also to have some mundane expertise. Astrology will only work best in medical matters when applied by doctors, in psychological matters by psychologists, in money matters by economists, in election forecasting by psephologists ...

There are moments in all our lives when our deep interest in some matter makes us minor prophets, epitomized most commonly perhaps when, in our expertise as parents, we see the mistakenness of some of the life decisions of our children while poignantly also knowing they must play out the consequences of their choices and learn their own lessons.

FACT VERSUS MEANING

In the realm of prophecy there is a principle analogous to Heisenberg's Uncertainty Principle: you can predict material reality, e.g. (during a particular time span), 'You are likely to need repairs to your home' *or* 'You will have some profoundly transformative emotional experiences', but not both combined. The same material facts can be experienced in vastly different ways by different people; the same subjective experience can be connected to vastly different external events. Mixing material and experiential truths leads to false inferences, false hopes and false fears. Macbeth's witches were evil by this criterion.

No astrologer worthy of the title imposes unsolicited predictions or prophecies on a client. But once a question has been asked in a context defined and articulated by the client, the astrologer has the ability to give a prediction consonant with the question's meaning for the questioner, and psychological completion of the relevant issue is achieved.

PAST, PRESENT AND FUTURE

Because the future, notwithstanding the best possible predictions, remains open, it is arguable that the greatest value of astrology lies in the understanding and appreciation it offers us of the past, which is already manifest.

Nevertheless, when our concerned preoccupations are narrowly focused, predictive astrology can be enormously valuable in informing us when present difficulties will pass and when desired and planned future events will probably be actualized.

When will my house, which has been on the market for six months, find a buyer? When will my present financial difficulties ease? When is the best time for nudging my reluctant lover into commitment? Should I change my career now and, if not now, when? When is a good time the next six months for me to have elective surgery? are all questions that an astrologer may confidently answer to particular clients, so offering them increased patience, acceptance, and serenity.

AN ASTROLOGICAL
EXPERIMENT

In 1984, under the supervision of the late Professor
Hans Eysenck, I designed and conducted an
experiment to test the truth of astrology. I advertised for
"skeptical but open-minded couples, married or in an
intimate living-together relationship", and the 122
respondents (61 couples) sent me their birth data. Based
on my interpretation of the synastry between the couples'
horoscopes, each individual was sent a description of how
he or she experienced his or her partner, together with
four dummy descriptions, and asked to rank the five
descriptions in order, from the most to the least true of
how they actually experienced their partners. Because of
the widespread awareness of the characteristics associated
with the sun-signs no reference was made to these in the
descriptions.

42 of the respondents put the correct descriptions in first
place and the overall results attested to the *existence* of
astrology at the 1% level of significance.

ASTROLOGY AND CAESAREAN BIRTHS

A legitimate doubt expressed to astrologers concerns the validity of the horoscopes of induced or Caesarean births. Are we not thereby interfering with nature and camouflaging its intent with our interference? I – and most astrologers – think not.

Notwithstanding that induced and Caesarean births are often associated with seemingly trivial contingencies such as the obstetrician's or surgeon's social arrangements, to the extent that an individual's determined nature is defined at the moment of conception, we may infer that the manner and time of her birth is part of that determinism.

Chinese horoscopes are drawn up in terms of the inferred time and date of conception (yet lead to interpretations congruent with those of Western horoscopes) so for them the justification I have given is very plausible. But for Western horoscopes, which are drawn for the moment of birth, the issue is more contentious and deserves some well-designed illuminating research.

ASTROLOGY AND TWINS

The horoscopes of twins are an interesting and special challenge to astrological understanding. From the testimonies of parents of twins, they often develop markedly dissimilar personalities even though their horoscopes are virtually identical. Sometimes the characteristics that non-astrologers see as hugely different are astrologically congruent. A prominent Neptune, for example, may prompt one twin to become a sailor, the other a photographer, both of which are Neptunian occupations. Another possibility is that they consciously or unconsciously divide their horoscope up between them, one living out one half of their horoscope's potential and the other living out another half.

Conversely, there is considerable evidence of amazing synchronicity in the lives of twins separated at birth as well as in the lives of unrelated time twins, from breaking their ankles at the same time and date on ski slopes miles apart to wearing identically idiosyncratic jewellery, to having same-named spouses and children.

WHERE CHOOSING IS HUBRIS

An electional chart is the horoscope of an entity such as the starting of a business, a marriage, the laying of a foundation stone, declaring war … whose moment of birth was explicitly chosen to create a 'best' horoscope for that entity. While it is arguable that such choices are no more than going with the tide, which is one of the best uses to which we can put astrology in daily life, I believe electional horoscopes are an act of hubris. Who are we to presume to know better than the cosmos what hand is best for a human being or any other entity to be dealt? This is quite different from wisely choosing moments to act in particular ways for an already existent entity.

I am, of course, making he same objection, in extended form, as the many people who object to our realizing the possibility of designer babies.

Deuteronomy

HERE AND NOW

SHAMEFULNESS AND SHAMELESSNESS

Hurry Up shame*less*ness has lately replaced Be Perfect shame*ful*ness in our culture. We need instead to gain and maintain an optimum balance between them. Eroticism in particular suffers from both excesses.

Shamefulness makes us overly inhibited about our sensuality in general and our sexuality in particular. Shamelessness reduces our sense of our selfhood and our sexuality to nothing but a material arrangement of organs and their functions and appetites, and destroys the possibility of experiencing sex as the sacred expression of love, in which expression it is the most ecstatic experience available to us in life.

Our contemporary shamelessness is an aspect of our technocracy. We liken our bodies to so many of our machines – toys that offer us ever speedier consummation of our desires, together with an addictive greed for ever more sophisticated techniques that we fantasize will give us the deep and lasting satisfaction that technology itself destroys.

THE BURDEN OF CHOICE

Today we are free shamelessly to be and to do anything we like: to be monogamous or polygamous, heterosexual or bisexual or homosexual, single or joint parents, to eat at home or in the street any time, to work sixteen hours a day or beg in the subway. The only taboo is against freedom of expression of opinion which we call Political Incorrectness. Society has become a lazy parent who, in the name of liberality, cruelly demands of the two-year old in each of us, 'vanilla, chocolate or strawberry?'

Wouldn't it be lovely if Paris once again dictated the length of our hemlines; we were not allowed to leave the table until everybody had finished; if we hid our deviances in willing hypocrisy, generally being obliged to conform, and thus freeing ourselves to concentrate on what really matters to us, encumbered by the mind-numbing demand of forever having to choose?

PERMISSIVENESS AND CYNICISM

The generations that have attained adulthood in the past thirty years or so have heard about the supreme joy of loving sexual intimacy and presume this to be intrinsic to the act of sex itself rather than as the earned expression of love that has been nourished. Previous generations were protected against this misunderstanding by the moral imperatives of religious education. Now, our permissive society is the enemy of joy in denying the need for pain or shame in intimate relationships and speciously denying the eternal battle of the sexes and the truce between them achieved by the art of sexual politics.

People have always transgressed sexual taboos but previously, when they were disappointed in the outcome of their transgressions, they could attribute their disappointment to their failure to live up to their own ideals. Now they can only feel the pain of cynical nihilism with no prospect of redemption.

PERMISSIVENESS AND DIVORCE

While the huge failure rate of contemporary marriages can plausibly be attributed, at least in part, to the freedom society grants us to part shamelessly, as previous generations could not, it is also partly attributable to the ease with which people 'have' sex. 'I fancy you' is very quickly consummated but, unromantically, in no way guarantees emotional compatibility.

Courtship, in the past, was the period in which couples eschewed full sexual congress and faced full frontally the challenges of their emotional differences and difficulties before deciding the rightness or wrongness of each other as marriage partners. Now couples can short-circuit their inevitable antagonisms by falling into bed and, in the absence of any other deeper understanding, many modern marriages are made on the basis of sexual habit. But sexual passion fades quickly, after which many couples discover their deep incompatibilities, the pain of which prompts them to divorce.

THE UNHAPPINESS OF MEN

Every culture shapes both genders to be recognizable to each other in their differences. As Jan (nee James) Morris bears witness: "Having in the second half of the twentieth century, experienced life in both roles, there seems no aspect of existence, no moment of the day, no contact, no arrangement, no response, which is not different for men and for women."

Contemporary men, no longer better than women as breadwinners, no longer valued as heroes for killing in the name of preserving wife, children and civilization and no longer heads of households, are now as unhappy as women were forty years ago. Out of their desolation they are ironically seeking self-esteem through the narcissism that women have rejected. Men's magazines flourish, promoting face creams and lifts and clothing to make men, like women, sexually desirable objects, their only alternative seemingly being a resort to brutish laddism. What will happen next?

THE POLITENESS OF
SEXISM

Of all the political incorrectness that are now taboo none is so joyless as that against sexism. The love-hate, push-pull of duality ambivalently seeking unity in the battle of the sexes infuses life with most of its colour and excitement, even counteracting our fear of death in the ecstasy it sometimes bestows on us. Men desire and women desire to be desired; but no longer may a man by touch or innuendo express his desire for a woman and no longer may a woman admit to enjoying a salacious remark or look given her by a man.

Far from undermining women true sexism is politeness of the soul. I once memorably observed an elegant young man flirting, to her obvious delight, with an obese old woman selling him a bunch of flowers from her market stall. Men, too, deserve charm and a 'no' that is grateful rather than gracelessly hostile.

MEN AND FAITHFULNESS

Women simply desire men's faithfulness; men complexly desire to have sex with many women *and* to be lovingly and securely cared for. Until recently women were united in their agreement to refuse men their sexual favours until they had feminized them by transmuting their lust into love. Men protested but were secretly glad to find in marriage the best possible resolution of their conflict. Notwithstanding their infidelities the vast majority of men have always chosen marriage over free promiscuity, realizing that in leaving a wife for a mistress the mistress quickly becomes another wife. In truth, of the four groups, married and unmarried women and married and unmarried men, bachelors are unhappier than married or single women and married men the happiest of all.

Now, in the name of liberation, women pretend that they too love sexual variety for its own sake and unhappily bemoan the unsurprising fickleness of men.

MEN, WOMEN AND CHILDREN

Men submit to the hard bargaining of women not only for sex and love, but also for the primary human need to feel useful.

Both boys and girls typically spend their childhoods in the female-dominated environments of home and school. Mothers are observably busy and useful, and a girl knows that, as a grown-up, she too will naturally be busy and useful. A boy, however, has only a vague perception of what it is his father does that he too will do when he is a man. He only knows that he must untie himself from his mother.

Thus young men avow and grow their masculine self-esteem by loudly banging their bongo drums in defiance of their feared emasculation. But then they realize they also need to be useful to others to feel good about themselves, which they can best achieve by becoming breadwinners for women and their shared children.

POPULATE OR PERISH?

By far the biggest change in human consciousness over the past 50 years has been the emergency of universal awareness of the world's population explosion. This was not the case even forty years ago. Especially in Australia, where I was then living, there was plenty of room for everybody and full employment, and government hoardings exhorted us to "populate or perish". Our individual existences were valued as useful to the collective, we know we were needed and so were full of buoyant self-esteem.

Now, we all know there are too many of us and the world could well do without us individually. Collectively, self-esteem is low, especially among the working classes whose unskilled labour no longer has value to the collective. In England, the working class Try hard-Be Strong personality, full of pride and dignity, has been replaced by the Try Hard-Hurry Up personality, full of pugnacious rage.

WAR, EXCITEMENT AND RIGHTEOUSNESS

Until lately in human history one of the chief balances of speed, excitement and adventure in our lives was the predictability, order and safety of religion and its prescribed rituals. Pilgrimages and holy wars provided participants with a satisfying blend of Hurry Up excitement and Be perfect discipline through the combination of the life-risking dangers of travel and war and the immutable conviction of righteous certainty in the name of God's will and protection. The latter-day equivalent is travelling in the name of Work, with lower levels of both commitment and excitement than en route to a Crusade but with a fair homeostatic balance maintained.

The recent rise in religious fundamentalism has been a bid to restore homeostasis in the face of the ever-increasing speed of contemporary life. Thus Hurry Up and Be Perfect have both risen to such escalated levels that they have imploded in the insanity of suicide bombers.

TOURISM AND EXCITEMENT

Tourism is now the world's biggest industry. It is a manifestation of our contemporary addiction to speed.

Travelling is a universally and timelessly popular means of satisfying our episodic needs for stepping outside the safe structure of our routine lives into speedy excitement. But implicit in the promises of travel is that the effort/planning we invest in the process of our travels is proportion to the pleasurable excitement of adventure and novelty that we achieve.

Before the invention of the steam engine and the bicycle the greatest attainable speed was that of a horse, and the best possible comfort and safety in a closed vehicle pulled by a horse over roads incomparably bumpier than our present-day worst. But a few miles travel could reward us with a novelty value – changed culture, changed dialect – that we now have to travel thousands of miles to achieve. We are fast running out of novel possibilities on earth – witness the recent first space tourist!

THE LIMITS OF
EXCITEMENT

The bombing of the World Trade Center on September 11th 2001 was, for most people, more than enough excitement, resulting in an immediate de-escalation of the Hurry Up quest for travel in favour of stay at home quietude. Soon after this horrific implosion of Be Perfect-Hurry Up insanity, fear of travel was further increased by the revelation of the life-threatening danger of deep vein thrombosis associated with air travel.

There are also gentler forces operating to de-escalate and redress the balance of Be Perfect and Hurry Up in our lives. There is continuing growth in the popularity of quiescent activities such as transcendental meditation, the self-discipline of perfecting our bodies at the gym, and obsessiveness about maintaining our health and fitness and prolonging our lives through diet and dietary supplements. Self-regulation of our homeostatic need to balance speed and calm, cautious self-discipline and adventurous spontaneity is beginning to gain ground.

TIME-SPEED ADDICTION

Our contemporary addiction to speed is an outgrowth of the products of technology. The bicycle, telegraph, telephone, internal combustion engine, aeroplanes, mobile phones, e-mail, the internet … give us convenience and comfort previously undreamt of, and – fortuitously – ever-increasing speed. So speed has become an addiction in our lives, a substance – like cigarettes or drugs – whose ingestion we are persuaded is the means to satisfying our appetite for time, but which provides only fleeting illusions of time gained while creating an ever-increasing craving for it.

Busyness dominates our lives, our diaries being fuller into the more and more distant future. Addictively we grasp for time in our specious bid to overcome the anxiety that our technological time-savers have created. The integrity of our nervous systems is at stake. Every new device for our greedy delectation is like another block on the tower of our being which is now precariously close to toppling.

STRAWBERRIES IN FEBRUARY

While much of our contemporary addiction to speed can be attributed to the speed that is intrinsically valued in the products of technology, some of it is also a compensation for the diminishment of our natural experiences of the seasons.

Central heating and air-conditioning make our lives optimally comfortable throughout the year; we are continuously offered a super-abundance of foods from throughout the world; and our gluttonous appetite for television cookery programmes testifies to our need for evermore sophisticated novelty in our daily food to compensate for the no longer existent pleasures of the limited seasonal availability of delicacies alike strawberries and asparagus, and the novelties of previously untried foods when we travelled abroad. Now, at home and abroad, high streets are swamped by multi-national chains purveying identical goods. And even the most fundamental physical adventures like climbing Mount Everest have been made almost safe, easy and commonplace.

FREEDOM VERSUS OBSERVANCE

Notwithstanding that by the beginning of the twentieth century religious fervor was rapidly declining in favour of passionate devotion to the wonders of science, habit died hard and most people still, however perfunctorily, regularly and dutifully attended places of worship. So, too, was non-religious daily life contained in Be Perfect timetabling of washing, ironing, cleaning, baking, visiting relatives, going for drives in the country … and most people ate fish on Fridays, roast beef and Yorkshire pudding on Sundays, and a very limited range of meals on other days of the week as well. Until the 1960s life was ritualized to an extent almost unbelievable to those too young to remember. The absence of choice bound everything in place through ceremony and continuity.

Only forty years on, nothing is prescribed or proscribed and virtually all observance – religious or secular – has dissolved in favour of the freedom and addictive delights attendant on our affluence.

WHEN WILL THE BALLOON BURST?

Since it took the first half of the twentieth century for the age-old habits of worshipful ritual and ceremony to die out in response to the death of God, it is likely to be some time yet before the now habitual quest for excitement and novelty dies out in the face of ennui. Fast food, fast cars, fast sex, fast money, fast divorce, and fast celebrity are still the order of the day. The Far East and the Antipodes have become *de rigeur* minimum requirements for European youth in search of their adventures, and such travel is commonplacely affordable. But today the news is of a second Space tourist who has paid £14,000,000 for the exclusively better, more distant and more exciting adventure of accompanying two astronauts on their scientific mission.

Is this where affordability will reach its limits for all but the mega-rich, and pleasure will be radically re-defined?

PROFESSIONALISM

A hundred years ago, in the absence of antibiotics and central heating, life was shorter and physically much more uncomfortable than today. Nevertheless, self-sufficiency was for most people possible most of the time; whereas today the sophisticated demands we have for our health, comfort and amusement feel like survival needs, and we are ever-more dependent on others to provide and maintain what have become essentials in our lives.

Thus was born professionalism, which is nurturing, reassuring know-how. We are all professionals now, each purveying some small Parent ego state expertise in response by the ever-expanding imperative Child needs that only others can satisfy. Implicit in nearly every payment we now make to another is the agitated cry, 'I'm helpless, make it better for me', from the TV repair man, to our personal trainers, gym instructors, hairdressers, plastic surgeons and financial advisers. Survival is ever more psychological and feels evermore frighteningly tenuous.

THE DISSOLUTION OF TRUST

Professionalism is a function of the Parent ego state, encompassing the balance of caring responsibility and autonomous authority. A hundred years ago there were few professions and the professionals there were – doctors, lawyers, teachers, and the clergy – were revered and trusted for their unquestionable integrity and selfless concern for the people they served.

Now that professionalism is democratized to include multitudes whose orientation is me-first Child rather than you-first Parent, we feel justified in *mis*trusting the plethora of servants we rely on to keep our cars, television, computers, plumbing, and roofs in states of repair; and we also call to account true professionals, discounting their authority and suspecting their integrity. Complaints procedures abound, professionals who touch those in their care risk being charged with criminal abuse, targets are set for doctors and teachers as if they were manufacturers of consumables.

No wonder doctors don't pay house visits any more.

THE AUTISM OF
SPECIALIZATION

Evolutionarily, we seem to be living at the critical time when our left brains have achieved parity with our right brains and we are embarking on an era of right and left brain synthesis which we can New Age thinking.

The twentieth century was one of increasing specialization in which people were required to know more and more about less and less in order to procure their PhD's and ensure their viability in the employment marketplace.

Now this situation is changing in a way that is both retrograde and progressive. In many subjects, knowledge has been particularized to its limits; and, perhaps more importantly for the general human condition, academics and others have become more and more unhappily isolated in their specialisms. The result is a burgeoning revival of inter-disciplinary conferences and cogent but popular writing about science that extends communication and nourishing strokes for intellectual givers and receivers alike.

Evolutionarily, our left-brains have achieved parity with our right-brains and we are embarking on an era of right – and left-brain synthesis which we call New Age thinking.

ANXIETY AND ADDICTION

Addictions express our bid to reduce our anxiety by behaviour which enlarges the anxiety that it momentarily diminishes. Anxiety is a component of both Be Perfect and Hurry Up, so the pervasiveness of drug addiction in the world today is consonant with the extreme Hurry Up-ness of contemporary life and the Be Perfect excesses that seek to balance it.

One third of the population of Britain still smokes cigarettes and, at any time, a quarter to a half of all the adults in the world are puffing at a cigarette. Smokers are polarized into Hurry Up types for whom smoking is one of their many self-destructive tendencies and the Be Perfect types who so fear being out of control that, notwithstanding that they know they are courting death by smoking – and hate themselves for this – continue to smoke for the momentary sense of control that the instant of inhaling grants them.

ANOREXIA NERVOSA

Anorexia nervosa is a disease of Be Perfect escalated to insanity. In the past it was idealized or vilified as ascetic sainthood or dangerous witchcraft. Contemporarily, it is rampant but, contrary to popular belief, it is phenomenally rather than essentially connected to the promotion of women's sexual desirability being contingent on thinness. Indeed, under the disguise of aiming for a cosmetically sexual ideal, it is a retreat from sexuality into pre-pubescent state of innocence. Fear of eroticized adulthood is converted into a food phobia and, food being a necessity for our physical survival, it has an approximately 25% mortality rate.

I believe the latter-day prevalence of anorexia nervosa is part of the Be Perfect backlash against the excesses of Hurry Up that are the hallmark of contemporary life; but, ironically, at the insane degree of Be Perfect that is anorexia nervosa it might just as well be Hurry Up.

MORAL RELATIVITY

The power of money-to-spend has turned Britain into a Child-led rather than a Parent-led culture.

Until about forty years ago children, generally without prompting, surrendered their seats on buses and elsewhere to adults; now they don't even do so for cripples. Teachers could count on the explicit endorsement of their authority by the parents of their pupils; now they are often abused and sometimes even physically attacked by some parents as well as children. Patients used to trust and revere the care and expertise of their doctors; now they sue them at the drop of a stethoscope.

Moral relativity is politically *de rigeur*. Adults are no longer consensually united in their moral values and codes of behaviour, leaving children – and the Child in all of us – anxiously bereft of the security of authoritative containment. Thus the streets of London are filthy and the lives of teachers, doctors and policemen hell.

THE ECLIPSE OF THE SUN

On August the 11th 1999 at 11.18am, together with about 20,000 other people, I stood on Plymouth Hoe and witnessed the first total eclipse of the sun visible from mainland Europe in 72 years. The shops all closed. As in days of yore, young, old, poor, rich, educated and ignorant became for a moment as one in response to the majesty of the cosmos.

The weather being overcast (as it so often is in England) and our human eyes being so cleverly adaptive, until the actual moment of totality the physical experience was merely that of a gloomy day. But when the 30 seconds of blackness arrived – exactly when predicted! – a roar of transcendental joy burst forth from the crowd. For that moment all separateness between people was lost. Not since the Moon Landing had I witnessed such a beautiful moment in which humanity was united in spiritual awe.

WAR, WISDOM AND EXPEDIENCY

At the time of writing (April 2002) the world is quailing in the face of terrorism, and moral debate rages concerning the righteousness and/or efficacy of bellicose retaliation.

In truth, punishment only suppresses undesirable behaviour while the punishment is being inflicted, but actually reinforces that behaviour, which escalates immediately the punishment is lifted. But, in practice, short-term expediency sometimes has to take precedence over wisdom, which is the justification given by America and Israel in their (Child to Child) wars on terrorism.

Wise parents leave their children to fight their own battles to completion, through which the children learn the interpersonal skills they will need throughout their lives, but when the threatened injury to either or both the belligerents is too great to be tolerated, parents feel bound powerfully to intervene. This is the (Parent to Child) role of America in its intervention in the war between Israel and Palestine.

WAR AND PSYCHOLOGY

When the Righteous Blamer (Israel) meets the Fighter of Lost Causes (the Arab nations) sparks inevitably fly. The Righteous Blamer is usually very clever and dominant due to the combination of its conviction of its superior morality and its pragmatic ability to maintain control of others through manipulation. The Fighter of Lost Causes is equally convinced of its moral rectitude, but this is combined with a perception of itself as inferior and a failure. Towards the Righteous Blamer, it is consumed with envious resentment and rage.

In open warfare between them, the Righteous Blamer will always win, but at great cost. To win peace, the Righteous Blamer must hide its dominance and pretend to forgo its righteousness. Patronage only further humiliates the Fighter of Lost Causes and escalates its rage to murder. Only when Israel has the *nous* to convey, 'You're right, we're wrong' can there be a safe, lasting armistice.

THE FUTILITY OF PUNISHMENT

Punishment does not work in its avowed aim and justification of curing the culprit of his misbehaviour. Punishment seems to work because the offending behaviour is momentarily suppressed while the punishment is being inflicted, but reasserts itself with added vigor the moment the punishment is lifted. The miscreant feels righteous, the punisher feels righteous. Righteousness is the root of all evil.

Praise (positive strokes) reinforces behaviour and makes the recipient feel good about him/herself; punishment (negative strokes) reinforces behaviour and makes the recipient feel bad about him/herself. People who feel good about themselves feel benevolent towards others and are liked; people who feel bad about themselves feel malevolent towards others and are disliked. Through the cult of retribution – in families, school, prisons, and between nations – the good get better and the bad worse.

Animal trainers have always known these facts. Why don't we elect animal trainers to be our leaders?

THE IDEAL OF PEACE

America as parent to the warring children of Israel and Palestine is threatening to stop their pocket money if they don't stop fighting. America is saying, 'Now both of you say sorry, kiss and be friends.' But what value have grudging, unfelt 'sorries'? The belligerents will be at each other's throats again the moment the parents turn their backs. So what can be done short of allowing the antagonists licence to unbridled mutual destruction?

Given the aggressive impulse in our human nature there is no hope of ever achieving continuous peace among people, barring an invasion by the Martians when we will be united in a war against them. The highest level of quasi-peaceful maturity attainable by human beings is the willingness to compromise, which means each of the parties saying, 'I'll give you some of what you want in exchange for you giving me some of what I want.'

STAR PEACE

B etween August 1002 and May 2002 the world was beset by a rarely occurring very challenging configuration in the heavens – Saturn opposing Pluto – which means that collectively, and for most individuals as well, we had to face some hard transformative challenges.

Saturn stands for conservatism, hard work, duty, obligation, fear, inhibition, burdens ... and Pluto stands for inexorable total revolution combined with an obsessive resistance to losing control, which is entailed in letting go of the past in favour of an as yet unpromised future. When these two forces clash they find expression in a tense mixture of frustration and anxiety, not uncommonly manifest in explosive violence.

As Pluto and Saturn separated at the end of May 2002, they gave way to some more than averagely easeful configurations in the sky lasting for the rest of 2002, associated with popular opinion tending to be increasingly against precipitate belligerence – at least for now.

MY DADDY

My Daddy (1911-2000) was a kind and gentle man. He was always quietly and calmly reassuring whenever I was frightened or hurt. He made me feel successful by teaching me to tie shoelaces the easy way (knot two loops) and do long-division in a quick way. And he took me on walks in the country and taught me, "Tell me, oh hen, oh when, when, when, will you lay me an egg for my tea?"

He made me feel loved and sweetly feminine, and in a completely non-sexist way encouraged me to be and do anything in the world I wanted, with only one precautionary (and heartfelt) warning, which I have always heeded; out of his experience as a raincoat manufacturer, he told me, "Never have stock!" Best of all, he conveyed to me his appreciation of and gratitude for everything he ever had in the world, material and non-material.

Rest in peace.

AMBROSIA

Enough thinking!

Melt 1 oz. butter, take off the heat and stir in 6 crushed digestive biscuits with a fork. Spoon into the base of a round buttered 8" spring-clip baking tin, pressing down firmly.

Break up and smooth 500 gm cottage cheese in a food processor. Separate 3 large eggs into separate bowls. Add 4 oz caster sugar to the yolks and beat with a wooden spoon until creamy and light. Add 1 oz cornflour and $\frac{1}{2}$ teaspoon of vanilla essence and beat until mixed thoroughly. Beat in the cheese and stir in 1 carton soured cream.

Whisk the egg whites until stiff then fold into the rest, gently but evenly. Pour the mixture into the tin and bake in the centre of a moderate oven (180C) for 1 hour. Turn off the oven and leave for a further 15 minutes. Allow to stand for 24 hours before devouring.

INDEX

Live Issues

Index